MEXICAN-AMERICAN CATHOLICS

PASTORAL SPIRITUALITY SERIES

MEXICAN-AMERICAN CATHOLICS

by

Eduardo C. Fernández

Paulist Press
New York/Mahwah, NJ

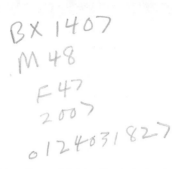
The Paulist Press Pastoral Spirituality Series is edited by Rev. Peter C. Phan, PhD, and Daniel Mulhall.

The Scripture quotations contained herein are from the New Revised Standard Version: Catholic Edition Copyright © 1989 and 1993, by the Division of Christian Education of the National Council of the Churches of Christ in the United States of America. Used by permission. All rights reserved.

Cover photo: *Increíble las Cosas q' Se Ven*, 1998, acrylic on brick, St. Pius V., Chicago. Painted by Jeff Zimmermann. Photo by Rev. Antonio (TJ) Martinez, Jr., SJ.

Cover design by Trudi Gershenov
Book design by Lynn Else

Library of Congress Cataloging-in-Publication Data

Fernández, Eduardo C.
    Mexican-American Catholics / by Eduardo C. Fernández.
        p.   cm.—(Pastoral spirituality series)
    Includes bibliographical references (p.   ).
    ISBN-13: 978-0-8091-4266-8 (alk. paper)
    1. Mexican American Catholics. 2. Catholic Church—Mexico—History.
I. Title.
BX1407.M48F47 2007
282'.730896872—dc22

                                                                    2007017458

Published by Paulist Press
997 Macarthur Boulevard
Mahwah, New Jersey 07430

www.paulistpress.com

Printed and bound in the
United States of America

CONTENTS

CONTENTS

INTRODUCTION
TO THE SERIES

The American Catholic Church is an "institutional immigrant" composed of many racial and ethnic groups with diverse religious and cultural traditions. It is also made up of churches that are not "Roman" or "Latin" but derive their religious and cultural heritage from the Orthodox Churches. Earlier groups, mostly from Western European countries, have by and large moved into the mainstream of American society and currently constitute the majority of American Catholics. Recent immigrants and refugees come from other parts of the world such as Asia, the Caribbean Islands, Eastern Europe, and Latin America. Together with the original native people who were present on the continent before the so-called discovery of the New World, these newcomers have dramatically swelled the ranks of the American Catholic Church. The native peoples and these newer immigrants and refugees—both documented and undocumented—are in many ways a blessing and boon for American society and the American Catholic Church. Recently the U.S. Conference of Catholic Bishops recognized the importance and contributions of these peoples in two statements, *Welcoming the Stranger Among Us: Unity in Diversity* (2000) and *Asian and Pacific Presence: Harmony in Faith* (2001). At the same time, both American society and the Church are facing difficult challenges with regard to these people who are, culturally and religiously, different from their European predecessors and quite diverse among themselves. Part of the difficulty lies in the absence of up-to-date and accurate information on these ethnic groups and their cultural and religious backgrounds.

To help the Catholic Church in the United States carry out its pastoral ministry to all people, Paulist Press is issuing the Pastoral Spirituality Series—books on the cultural and religious heritages of many of these ethnic groups in the Roman as well as Eastern Catholic Churches of America. The ultimate aim of these books is to promote communion in the Church, a communion that recognizes and celebrates the diversity of God's blessings in the ethnic, racial, sociopolitical, sexual, religious, and cultural richness that all peoples bring to the United States. Such a communion eschews uniformity, and yet seeks to maintain and develop the unity in faith, hope, and love in the service of God's reign.

The publisher, authors, and editors of this series fervently hope that these books will contribute to a better understanding of and appreciation for the unique cultural and religious heritages these communities bring with them to share with the Church in the United States. In the long run, their presence will forge a new type of America and a new model of Church.

Peter C. Phan
Series General Editor

PREFACE

In June 2005 the Mexican government opened its forty-sixth consulate in the United States of America in St. Paul, the capital of Minnesota. An area known more for its Scandinavian roots than its Mexican flavor, St. Paul now boasts "22 churches offering services in Spanish, 9 Spanish-language newspapers, 3 tortilla makers and 9 Hispanic—mostly Mexican—soccer leagues."[1] The next scheduled consulate site is Little Rock, Arkansas.

As these examples illustrate, Mexicans are now migrating to places previously uninhabited by them. As the saying goes, "Vamos donde hay chamba" (We go where there is work). Minnesota's unemployment rate of 3.3 percent, together with that of several other states looking for less expensive manual labor, is definitely an attraction for inhabitants of the country south of the Rio Grande, which has had more than its share of problems adjusting to a global economy. What happens once these Mexicans start coming to U.S. parishes often not equipped to accommodate these newcomers?

This book is designed to be an introduction to ministry with and among Mexicans and Mexican-Americans. As a Mexican-American myself, having had three of my grandparents born in Mexico and die in the United States of America (to distinguish it from the United States of Mexico, its formal name), I have observed, written, and taught classes about our history, socioeconomic situation, theology, worship, pastoral practice, and spirituality for more than a decade. In order to prepare this book I have revisited my writings and brought them up to date, and developed new materials based on information obtained from the 2000 U.S. Census and from the oral wisdom of many laypeople, religious women and men, and priests who serve as pastoral agents.

Each chapter opens with a folk saying, or *dicho*. My grandmother, Abuela Emilia Carrasco, and my aunt, Tía Amparo Mendoza, taught me the wisdom of this type of speech, especially for persons who could not read or write. For centuries, people have turned to their proverbs in time of need and tribulation. "En tus apuros y afanes, acude a tus refranes" (In time of need, turn to your proverbs).[2] In preaching and teaching, I have been amazed by their ability to summarize and keep alive great human insights, thus providing "guidelines for the development of attitudes, moral values, and social behavior."[3]

The chapters that follow present this material along with sources that the pastoral minister can consult to further understand this very large, diverse group. Chapter 7 and the notes, found at the end of the text, will provide the reader with the source material consulted for this volume.

One of the frustrations in writing a book like this one, so comprehensive in scope, is the realization that one is forced to make certain generalizations that will have many exceptions, either because of geography, social class, generational differences, or simply the changing times. If I have succeeded in raising questions that will help foster a humble, listening ear versus providing simple, pat answers, I will have done my job.

It would be wrong for us Mexican-Americans to assume that we know our own culture, much less our emerging theology or the spirituality behind it. After all, sometimes as ministers the best we can do is trudge along the

Lord's highways and byways, confident that the gospel message has a power all its own.

A Word on Terminology: Throughout the text I use the words *Hispanic, Latino,* and *Latina* interchangeably. While each term has its own nuance, the usage is still quite flexible in common parlance. Because Mexicans make up the majority of the U.S. Hispanic population (approximately 64 percent), I often generalize to Mexicans what is said about Hispanics in general. A more complex distinction needs to be made between Mexicans and Mexican-Americans. But because Mexican-Americans are most often the children and later offspring of Mexican immigrants, this division does not always work and for this lack of clarification, I beg the reader's forgiveness and understanding.

In many ways, this work is a product of *pastoral de conjunto,* pastoral theology done as a group. From the friends, former students, and colleagues who collected articles and newspaper clippings for me, to those who were gracious enough to grant me an interview, to those research assistants who sought out materials, to those who let me use their written material, to those who simply provided an encouraging word when I was ready to scrap the project, I was blessed with many faithful companions. More specifically, I wish to acknowledge Anne Grycz, Timothy Matovina, Lauren Guerra, Edilberto López, Dorothy Peterson, FCJ, Allan Figueroa Deck, SJ, Roberto and Juanita Fernández, Joseph Doyle, SJ, Ponchie Vasquez, OFM, Peter Brown, Timothy Godfrey, SJ, Sean Carroll, SJ, Kim Mallet, Sylvia Chacón, ASC, Ann Francis Monedero, OSF, Jerome Baggett, Gustavo Pérez, Yolanda Tarango, CCVI, Eduardo Calderón, SJ, Kenneth McGuire, CSP, Ronald González, SJ, Ronald Boudreaux, SJ, Juan Carlos Pulido, and Sandra Torres. I would also like to thank the Lily Foundation, which provided the sabbatical research fellowship, through the

Association of Theological Schools (ATS), which allowed me to do the research during the academic year of 2003–4. My gratitude for their guidance and encouragement for this project also goes to Peter Phan, the editor of the Paulist Pastoral Spirituality Series, and Daniel S. Mulhall, series managing editor. Finally, I dedicate this book to my brother Jesuits who make up the Society of Jesus. As friends in the Lord, they not only provided me with an excellent education but also taught me to listen to the great desires of my heart. *¡Muchísimas gracias, hermanos en Cristo!*

Chapter 1

ORIGINS OF THE MEXICANS

A Brief Overview of Thirty Centuries of Mexican Religious History

Dios los hace y solitos se juntan.
(God creates them and then they get together on their own.)

Unlike modern cultures, which tend to look to the future, to "progress" often seen as "the latest and the fastest," traditional cultures have their gaze more fixed on the past. For this reason, in trying to grapple with the complexity of the Mexican culture, there is no substitution for studying its history. Mexican-American Catholics are a proud people descended from Aztec, Mayan, and other indigenous civilizations, whose history of Spanish colonization brought with it both exploitation and, gradually, over the centuries, valuable religious, cultural, and economic developments. Even the poorest campesino working today in the vineyards of Napa in the wine country region of northern California possesses an appreciation for this intricate history of both struggle and survival amid great difficulties. This chapter briefly outlines the complex history of the Mexican nation viewed particularly through the perspective of its social and religious institutions.

While traveling throughout Mexico, as with other ancient civilizations, one cannot but be struck by the number of religious monuments—whether pyramids, churches, or commemorative structures on hilltops—that are scattered throughout the republic. Even the bus terminals are not exempt, as it is not uncommon to see shrines there, especially ones devoted to Our Lady of Guadalupe. The Mexicans have always been an extremely religious people—religion and religious fervor did not arrive with the Spaniards—and no account of their history is credible if it does not take this spiritual fervor into account. Chapter 3, which focuses on Mexican spirituality, further describes this religiosity. This historical overview presents the role that formal religion plays in the development of a nation.

The Pre-Columbian Era

During 1990 and 1991 an art exhibit entitled "Mexico: Splendors of Thirty Centuries" toured several cities in the United States of America. This claim of thirty centuries was hard for U.S. Americans to accept. For such a relatively young country where anything more than fifty years old is considered an antique, the mention of a history of thirty centuries attributed to a country immediately south of its borders seemed, indeed, like a tall order. But the fact remains that not only was Tenochtitlán, the large Aztec city that the Spaniards came upon in 1519 and that is today the center of Mexico City, founded in 1325, but its founding drew plentifully upon an already centuries-old rich cultural heritage of the Aztec Empire. Theories of the origin of humans on American soil describe a human migration from the Asian continent, most likely beginning about 35,000 years ago via the then frozen Bering Strait. Human traces have been found in Mexico that date from about 20,000 BC.

One can divide the development of the country geographically into two regions, north and south. The more arid northern part is composed of what is now the part of the United States of America that includes the states of California, Arizona, New Mexico, and Colorado, and the present Mexican states of Baja California, Sonora, Chihuahua, Coahuila, Durango, and Zacatecas. The early inhabitants of these lands, predominantly hunters and fishers, did not establish large cities.

The southern portion, what is today known as Mesoamerica, produced several important urban cultures, the Aztec being the last of these before the arrival of the Spanish in the early sixteenth century. Of the various great civilizations that flourished in Mexico prior to the Aztecs, the oldest is the Olmec, located near the Gulf Coast, in the lowlands of what is now southern Veracruz and nearby Tabasco. Among its major cities are today's San Lorenzo, Veracruz, La Venta, and Tres Zapotes. These cities flourished from 1200 to 500 BC. These cities—distinguished by a design that included ceremonial buildings erected along a north-south axis—mark a notable shift from a rural to a more urban form of life. Perhaps the most famous images left behind by this great civilization are the large carved stone heads, the tallest one discovered measuring ten feet high.

The Olmec left much more than carvings, however. The Mexican historian Ignacio Bernal points out that the mathematical concept of the zero is an Olmec innovation, correcting the mistaken notion that the concept was created by the Mayans.[1] The many other notable contributions of the Olmecs, including those in trading, social organization, art, and religion, greatly influenced later civilizations.

Visitors to the valley of Mexico City today are often struck by the immensity of the pyramids located about an hour's bus ride from the center of the city. In a sense, this is all that remains of the great Teotihuacán, whose name means "the city of the gods" or "the place where gods are made." The larger of the two major pyramids, the Pyramid of the Sun, rises to a height of 216 feet. This city, with an estimated population of 125,000 people at its high point (AD 250–600), dates back to the beginning of the Christian era and, for its day, was probably among the most populated cities in the world. This advanced civilization had writing and books, the bar-and-dot number system, and the 260-day sacred year. This civilization was sacked by invading Toltecs sometime between AD 650 and 900.

Again, as with the Olmecs, a previous generation passed on to its conquerors much of its tradition, technology, and religious beliefs and symbols. For example, many of its gods, such as the feathered serpent Quetzalcóatle, a symbol of fertility and life, and Tláloc, the god of rain and water, were still being worshipped by the Aztecs more than a thousand years later.

Given a centralist tendency to focus much of the history of Mexico on the capital, before and after the Spanish conquest, the importance of the Mayan civilization is often underestimated. As early as AD 250, the Mayan people of the Yucatán Peninsula and the Petén forest of Guatemala were already building elaborate temple pyramids. In fact, by 1500 BC, they were settling into villages and cultivating corn (maize), beans, and squash. Throughout their classical period (AD 250–900), they distinguished themselves for their political alliances, elaborate art (which included the working of gold and copper), architecture, a system of writing, a further development of the calendar, and their knowledge of astronomy (they were able, for example, to predict eclipses of the sun and the movements of the moon and Venus). Over the centuries this civilization composed of city-states covered the area of the Yucatán, Campeche, and Guatemala, and went as far south as Honduras and northern Belize. Their nearly forty cities ranged in population from five thousand to fifty thousand, each containing elaborate temples, palaces, ball courts, and plazas.

Toward the end of the eighth century, the trade between these Mayan cities lessened and tensions surfaced. After AD 900, for reasons not entirely clear, the classical civilization declined (some archeologists attribute this decline to armed conflicts coupled with the exhaustion of arable land). Whatever the case, the great cities and ceremonial centers (whose ruins today remain astounding) were eventually abandoned. Most of their inhabitants migrated to the northern area or to the highlands of Chiapas. When the Spanish arrived in the early sixteenth century, the Mayans were basically village-dwelling agriculturalists who still practiced the religious rites of their ancestors.

While there are other notable civilizations that developed in the Mesoamerican region prior to the arrival of the Europeans, such as that of the Toltecs, we focus on the Aztecs, whose large empire, centered in what today is downtown Mexico City, was amassed through military strength. According to legend, the Aztecs saw themselves as the chosen people of their tribal god, Huitzilopochtli.

Originally snake eaters and inhabitants of peripheral swamp land, the Aztecs, with the help of their allies, eventually controlled thirty-eight provinces with an estimated population of 5 million people at the height of their empire in an area about the size of modern-day Italy. As rulers of an empire that demanded tributes from the tribes they had conquered, the Aztecs were, like the Romans, much hated by their subjects. In writing their history decades later, the

Aztecs speak of a sign received from the heavens that revealed to them where they were to build their great city. This sign, an eagle devouring a snake while perched on a cactus, is the symbol still found on the Mexican flag.

Inheritors of the artistic and architectural wisdom of previous Mesoamerican civilizations, the Aztecs built an incredible city, Tenochtitlán, which in the early sixteenth century probably had a population of 200,000 in what some have called the American Venice. Expanding from the islands in Lake Texcoco, in the heart of the city, they built an intricately designed city complete with a system of irrigation for farming, terracing, and swamp reclamation. In addition, they had a way of bringing freshwater to the heart of the city, which could only be reached by causeways. Bernal Díaz del Castillo, a chronicler of the Spanish conquest, records the initial impression of the Spaniards when confronted with these architectural accomplishments:

> and when we saw so many cities and populated valleys in the water and other great towns on dry land and that straight level causeway leading to Mexico, we were amazed and said that it was like the enchantments told of in the legends of Amadís because of the lofty towers and buildings, all of masonry, rising from the water. Some of the soldiers even said that it must be all a dream. It is not surprising that I write in this way because there is so much to think about that I do not know how to describe it, seeing things never heard of or even dreamed about.[2]

Like some of their predecessors, the Aztecs practiced human sacrifice. They believed that their god, the sun, needed human blood to stay alive. If the sun had human blood, it could then give warmth and therefore provide for all of human existence. If they wanted the sun to take care of them, then they had to take care of the sun. Often the blood offered came from a member of a conquered tribe. While the Spaniards were quick to condemn such practices, viewing them as demonic, the Dominican missionary and great defender of the indigenous people Fray Bartolomé de las Casas pointed out its Christological parallel: Jesus, too, offers himself up and the best thing a Christian can do is to offer his or her life so that others may live.[3]

Before describing the mentality of the Spaniards who came to conquer, we draw several conclusions from this brief overview of the indigenous civilizations that preceded the European presence in Mesoamerica.

First, the native populations were not monolithic. There existed not only many cultural and linguistic differences between the various tribes, but also many political ones. Hernán Cortés, the Spanish commander, used these differences and rivalries to his great advantage.

Second, because of its rich, nearly three thousand years of history, Mexican civilization was highly complex, having produced written, technological, philosophical, and religious innovations.

Finally, as the cult of Quetzalcoatl demonstrates, their religious beliefs exhibited an astonishing degree of tenacity. They were an extremely religious peoples and one of the most demoralizing factors of the conquest for them was to have their religious systems destroyed.

The Spaniards who came to the Americas were also extremely religious; some might have been religious fanatics. At the time Columbus was encountering the New World in 1492, King Fernando and Queen Isabela of Spain, having united their kingdoms militarily, were now banishing or demanding the conversion of Spanish Jews and Muslims in an attempt to unify their kingdom religiously. Thus, the mentality of the *reconquista,* the taking back from the Muslims what had previously been parts of Christendom, was in the air. Spanish cities, such as Toledo, which had enjoyed religious toleration now found themselves subject to this new legislation. Besides the *reconquista* mentality there was also the feeling that, given the terrible loss that the Roman Church was suffering in Europe during the time of the Protestant Reformation (Luther having nailed his ninety-five theses to the door of the Wittenberg, Germany, church in 1517), Spain would be the great defender and promoter of the Catholic faith, even in the New World. More will be said about this initiative after a summary of the bloody conquest.

The Conquest and Early Evangelization

One of the most frequently asked questions about this moment in history is how the conquistador Hernán Cortés, who in 1519 arrived in Mexico with only eleven ships, 550 men, and sixteen horses, was able to defeat in only two short years such a powerful empire as that of the Aztecs. As already mentioned, the empire had many enemies. The defeated tribes were eager to assist the Spanish, anxious to defeat the Aztecs who exacted tribute from them. These tribes were unaware that they would soon suffer the same fate as the lords of the valley of Mexico. Also, given the inter-Spanish political intrigue that ensued after his landing, Cortés was able to win more soldiers to his side, having at his disposal about two thousand men and, according to his own writings, fifty thousand indigenous allies. In addition to the brutal force of war, the Spaniards also brought with them many European diseases, such as smallpox and measles. Having no biological resistance to these new ailments, the indigenous peoples sickened and died. Starting in

1520, dangerous epidemics quickly reduced the Indian population by 90 percent.[4]

Another factor that allowed the Spaniards to triumph was the superiority of their weapons. The indigenous people were simply horrified by the power of canons and muskets. Also contributing greatly to the fall of the Aztec Empire were the psychological warfare tactics employed by the Spanish. According to Aztec legend, they expected the god-king Quetzalcoatl to return from the east at about the time the Spaniards arrived. Because the god-king was supposed to be light-skinned, the ruler of the Aztecs, Moctezuma II, wondered if Cortés might indeed be the expected one. Moctezuma's army was very demoralized by the thought that they were fighting against gods. Cortés took advantage of this belief. The dramatic events that followed cannot be detailed here but suffice it to say that Cortés, overcoming a series of initial defeats and with the aid of his allies, captured the great city of Tenochtitlán in 1521. The Spaniards renamed this city "Mexico" and called their new colony "Nueva España" (New Spain). The importance of the apparitions of Our Lady of Guadalupe during this time will be discussed in the section on spirituality in chapter 3. For now, the most important thing to remember is that Our Lady comes to comfort and defend a brutalized indigenous population.[5]

Soon after the fall of Tenochtitlán, Cortés, suspicious of the secular clergy in Spain, asked the king of Spain, Charles V, to send Franciscan friars to begin the process of evangelization.[6] In 1523, the first three Franciscans, originally from Belgium, arrived in Mexico, the most famous of these being Fray Pedro de Gante (d. 1572), a lay brother related to the king, who is remembered for his great love and respect for the indigenous cultures. Together with the twelve Franciscans who were sent a year later, these early missionaries were very creative in their approach to the evangelization of the indigenous peoples. Schooled in the humanistic trend at the time represented by such thinkers as Erasmus (d. 1536) and Thomas More (d. 1535), they placed a great deal of importance on learning the language and culture of the people and sacred Scripture. They were convinced that the indigenous people would be drawn to Christianity if the Spaniards and the missionaries showed them Christ-like humility rather than using force. In those early years, Christian texts were translated into the native languages and preserved. The education of indigenous leaders was encouraged. The friars often attempted to show the compatibility of indigenous and Christian beliefs.

Overall, there was a sense that even though the spirit of early Christianity had been corrupted in Europe, the New World would provide a setting where its spirit could be reinstated. Prophetic persons such as Dominican Fray Bartolomé de las Casas (d. 1566), who denounced indigenous rights violations in the courts of Spain, and Bishop Vasco de Quiroga (d. 1565), who pioneered utopian-type craft cooperatives in what is today the region of the state of Michoacán, believed that, if Christianity were to be credible, it had to respect the local culture and help provide for the physical well-being of persons. Unfortunately, the conquerors did not share the same feeling. De las Casas wrote that because of their mistreatment at the hands of the Spaniards the native people felt that if Spaniards went to heaven, then they would prefer to go to hell.

In 1527, the first diocese was erected in Tlaxcala, New Spain (near Mexico City), the first bishop being Fray Julián Garcés, a Dominican. In the spirit of de las Casas, he was convinced of the full humanity of indigenous peoples. However, in the area of evangelization, he differed from Cortés, who, like another famous Franciscan, Fray Toribio de Benavente (named by the natives "Motolinia," meaning the "poor one"), favored baptism first and then evangelization. Both Garcés and Motolinia (who sided with Cortés) were concerned with the salvation of the people of the New World. Their method of evangelizing, however, was radically different.

In 1537, Pope Paul III published a bull entitled *Sublimis Deus* in which he recognized the full humanity of the indigenous peoples, and insisted that since they were rational beings and made to be free, they could not be deprived of their liberty or their goods. They were to be evangelized in the manner of Christ, the apostles, and the great missionaries of the Church. A few years before, in 1528, a bishop had been named for the city of Mexico. Fray Juan de Zumarraga, a Franciscan Basque, was also of the Erasmian humanist school. He was convinced that the evangelization of the Mexicans must follow the example of Christ and place religion at the service of people. He introduced the first printing press in all of the Americas, which printed the first catechism for the instruction of the indigenous peoples (one that had come out of what is today the Dominican Republic). Its novel approach favored a more biblical and narrative method over one that was more traditional, Scholastic, and analytical. The bishop of Mexico clearly chose a more inculturated approach.[7] The faith was to be explained not as a series of theological concepts but as the history of salvation. Similar innovations in the area of architecture, such as the open air chapels, responded to the need to catechize a large population and administer the sacraments.[8] The Mexican historian Alejandra Moreno Toscano summarizes the contributions of the missionaries:

> These missionaries left their imprint not only on the architecture of their monasteries but on many other aspects of the life of the region. During the sixteenth century they constructed hydraulic engineering

works, large dams, and complex irrigation systems in central and western Mexico (Yuriria), some of which are still in use today; they also introduced the cultivation of certain types of vegetables and fruit trees. Because it fell to the missionary and the priest to direct the community activities and define the new form of social organization of these conquered people, they soon became the hub of Indian life.[9]

In terms of the method of evangelization, the second half of the sixteenth century was not especially innovative. Following the Council of Trent (1545–63), the concern for orthodoxy loomed large, stemming from conflicts with the Protestant Reformation in Europe and the possibility of syncretism among the neophytes in the New World. In comparison to the Franciscan, Dominican, and Augustinian friars who proceeded them, the secular priests who came to Mexico following the early evangelization were not as skilled or interested in learning indigenous languages, hence emphasis was now placed on the indigenous populations learning Spanish. One of the most critical decisions made during this time was the decision not to ordain indigenous men to the clergy. This decision, which affected Latin America greatly then and the results of which are still felt today, was made because the native men were perceived as not being able to comply with celibacy nor deemed reliable enough to serve as agents of the Spanish state. As a result, for centuries most of the Mexican clergy were foreign-born or criollo, the name given to the children of Spaniards born in the Americas. It was not until the second half of the nineteenth century that a mestizo clergy finally emerged. Furthermore, it is not until the early twentieth century, when laws were passed to expel foreign clergy, that local Church leadership was transferred to the native clergy.

The Colonial Period

One the most influential forces shaping this period in Mexican history was the system of *patronato real,* or royal patronage. Because the king of Spain was in charge of the mission of evangelization in New Spain (Mexico) the Spanish Crown supported the Church economically and had the final word on what type of leadership was sent to the colonies. Church and state were one, and in many ways the Church functioned as a branch of the state. This state subsidy enabled the Church to build many majestic churches that, even today, remain artistic national treasures. While the state financed missionary campaigns, the Church assumed many of the social obligations of the colony such as education, health, and even law enforcement—which was carried out through the Inquisition. The result was that increasingly the decisions of the Crown weighed heavily upon the activities of the Church.

The last of the major religious orders to come to New Spain were the Jesuits, who arrived in 1572. Sent to evangelize the indigenous peoples, they soon found their educational services requested in many of the major cities. They quickly discovered themselves to be the primary educators of the criollos. Notwithstanding, they sponsored many missions, particularly in the northwestern parts of the colony, Pimería Alta, which today encompasses the U.S. state of Arizona and the Mexican state of Sonora, together with Baja California. The Jesuits had the advantage of being able to learn from what the previous orders had done before their arrival in Mexico, and many continued the task of evangelization following a strategy of inculturation in terms of language, symbols, and religious organizations. Like the great Franciscan friar Bernardino Sahagún, who wrote detailed studies of indigenous religious customs, ceremonies, and practices, the Jesuits continued the trend of learning the native cultures and even producing dictionaries and histories. They also helped the criollos to forge a national identity. The Jesuits were pro-Indian, the Creole Jesuit Pedro José de Márquez maintaining that "true philosophy does not recognize that any man has less ability because he was born white or black or because he was educated at the poles or in the tropics."[10] Similarly, Francisco Xavier Clavijero, who wrote a history of Mexico, was convinced that the Indians "were just as capable of learning all the sciences" as the Europeans.[11] Having instilled in many of their students an intellectual liberalism, the Jesuits educated many of the Creoles who eventually led the 1810 revolution against Spain to secure Mexican independence.

From Independence through Nationhood to the Present

Although it is impossible to do justice to the various important movements and events involving the history of the Mexican Church during this period, there are several conclusions that can be made. For one, the Church and state were involved in a bitter power struggle against a three-century tradition of the *patronato real*. The newly formed government sought to control the Church while the Church looked elsewhere, specifically to Rome, for leadership (most concretely in the direct naming of bishops). In a way, the conflict between the two groups resulted from the modern understanding of the separation of church and state. For example, when the state assumes more prominent control of the civil registry it becomes the state's responsibility (and not the church's) to sanction and record registry of births, marriages, and deaths. Mexicans who do not want to be affiliated with the Catholic Church may still have their children's births recorded, their marriages solemnized, and their dead buried. Thus, the freedom of religion is guaranteed.[12] Throughout the history of modern Mexico, the extent to which the Church was able to own land and exist as a corporation was hotly debated. Since colonial times it had acquired much wealth, but was also responsible for most of the social services people needed, such as education, health, and to a certain extent, judicial responsibilities (the Inquisition). With the emergence of a modern state, the government began to assume more of these functions. The Church, rightly concerned about past government abuses, but also about conserving its own wealth and privileges, was not exempt from politics. Those priests who led the independence revolution against Spain, for example, were excommunicated and tried by the Church. Similarly, during the U.S.-Mexican War, which lasted from 1846 to 1848, the Church refused to lend money to the Mexican government toward its defense against invading U.S. troops. At the end of that war, Mexico lost about half of its territory to the United States of America.

During the nineteenth century two political currents took center stage in Mexico: the conservative party, which favored a centralist government with strong ties to the Church, and a liberal party, which supported a federation of states, similar to that of the United States of America, one in which church and state remain separate and the actions of the Church are regulated by the state. Because both the liberals and the conservatives tried to control the Church, the Church had problems with both. In the eyes of the liberals— among them Benito Juárez, who rose to the presidency and ousted the emperor, Maximilian of Hapsburg (who had been imposed by Napoleon III of France during the 1860s)—there were two institutions that were in the way of a modern Mexico: the indigenous communal lands, known as *ejidos,* which went against the modern notion of private land ownership, and the Church. He and the other liberals, therefore, set out to dismantle the strength of both. Indigenous lands were expropriated and sold to individuals, and the Church's wealth was similarly nationalized.

In the hopes of making Mexico a modern nation modeled after its northern neighbor, the liberals allowed for an alternative way of being Christian in Mexico, that is, Protestantism. Perceived as being free from dogmatism and more respectful of individual conscience, especially as seen in the personal interpretation of Scripture, it was held up as a better mindset for advancing business and technology, as actualized in the prosperity of both the United States of America and England. The first Protestant missionaries to enter Mexico were the Methodists who, imbued with a social gospel mentality, contributed to social advancement through such means as education. Other Protestant groups, particularly those with roots in the United States of America, followed suit and continue to arrive in Mexico to the present day, the most recent being Pentecostals and evangelicals.

During the nineteenth century, according to the Constitution of 1857, the Church was tolerated but did not have juridical rights. It was not until the second half of the twentieth century, under the presidency of Carlos Salinas de Gortari (1988–94), that its juridical existence was sanctioned and laws curtailing the exercise of religion were removed from the books. Ironically, it was during this period of persecution by the state, roughly from the time of the 1857 Laws of Reform to the present era, that a mestizo clergy took root in Mexico, a trend not as common in many other Latin American countries. By curtailing the powers of the Church and refusing to allow foreign clergy to function in Mexico, the state unintentionally helped to bring about a more Mexican Church, one in which several significant Mexican religious communities of women and men flourished and, even to this day, are sending missionaries to other countries.

In the 1920s and 1930s, Church-state conflicts in Mexico came to a boil as the social revolution, which started in 1910 with the ouster of the dictator Porfirio Díaz, vied with the Church for the allegiance of the peasants. Díaz, who ruled the country for over thirty years, had been friendly to foreign businesses and large landowners. As peasants progressively began to lose more of their land, even that devoted to subsistence farming, their cry under the leadership of such revolutionaries as Emiliano Zapata and Pancho Villa became "Tierra y libertad!" (Land and Liberty!). In 1910 Francisco Madero led a revolt against the dictatorship of Díaz. After some months of fighting, united with the forces of Zapata and Villa, Madero's troops achieved a decisive victory in the battle of Ciudad Juárez in 1911. Díaz resigned in May and went into exile. Backed by a coalition of both urban and rural factions, Madero assumed the presidency. He was not able, however, to maintain a united government. Madero and his vice president were murdered, and the revolutionary forces split into contending factions. It was not until 1920, after several contenders had been eliminated, that the victors began cautiously to implement some of the social and agrarian reforms that had been promised in the Constitution of 1917.

Yet, when the tragic decade from 1910 to 1920 was over, about one-tenth of Mexico's citizens had lost their lives in a bloody revolution and many still had not achieved that for which they had sacrificed so much. During that same period the Church, primarily in the spirit of Pope Leo XIII's *Rerum Novarum* (1891), was becoming more committed to the rights of workers in a country that was increasingly industrialized.

When Plutarco Elías Calles became president in 1924, he continued the process of land distribution and inaugurated an ambitious program of public works and fiscal reform. While his predecessor, Alvaro Obregón, generally ignored the anticlerical articles of the 1917 Constitution, Calles was determined to enforce them. He forbade religious processions and closed Church schools, convents, and monasteries. Furthermore, he required that Mexican priests register with the civil authorities.

On July 31, 1926, the Mexican hierarchy retaliated against this political oppression by suspending religious services throughout Mexico. Catholic leaders in Michoacán, Puebla, Oaxaca, Zacatecas, Nayarít, and the backcountry of Jalisco began organizing the Catholic population to oppose the anticlerical government in Mexico City. Two prominent laymen, Anacleto González Flores and René Capistran Garza, led the resistance in the cities. General Enrique Gorostieta assumed leadership of guerrilla groups in the countryside. Because their cry was "Viva Cristo Rey!" they became known as the Cristeros. Their strategy was to attack government military outposts. The Cristeros were not able to defeat the federal army nor was the army able to suppress them. When Calles's term expired in 1928, the Cristeros still posed a threat to the revolutionary government. The situation was at a stalemate.

U.S. Ambassador Dwight Morrow played an important role in the negotiations that followed. He arranged meetings with Calles, Emilio Portes Gil (the new president of the republic), and Father John Burke, an influential Catholic leader in the United States of America. In order to ensure participation of the Mexican bishops in the negotiations, Morrow facilitated the return of some of them to Mexico. Most of the prelates were either in exile or in hiding. By June 1929, Church and state leaders reached a compromise. The hierarchy agreed to submit to the civil registration of priests and to refrain from protesting the prohibition of religious education in the schools. Government officials stated that their aim was not to destroy the Catholic Church in Mexico. They allowed for religious instruction, provided that it was held only in churches. The bishops ordered the Cristeros to lay down their arms. Priests were told to resume religious services.

The history of the Cristero Rebellion, as it has come to be called, is a complex one, much of which is still being written. At least in theory, the Mexican Church gave its approval to these rebellions, some of whose casualities included rural schoolteachers, and later, once they had laid down their arms, many Cristeros themselves. Beyond the simplistic categories of black and white, good and bad, this history, although undoubtedly filled with heroic stories, such as those of martyrs like Blessed Miguel Agustín Pro, SJ, must address to what extent such factors as peasant unrest and Church resistance and its boycott of religious services because of government persecution played a significant role in its escalation.

In comparison to the Church in other Latin American countries today, where, incidentally, often there are fewer native clergy, the Church in Mexico is more politically and theologically conservative. At a time when the anticlerical laws were still in place, the visit of Pope John Paul II to Mexico in 1979 demonstrated beyond the shadow of a doubt that the Church, which had the ability to bring people together en masse, was a powerful force. However, in the spirit of Vatican II and Puebla, the site in Mexico where the pope opened this important meeting of the Latin American bishops (Consejo Episcopal de America Latina, or CELAM), there has been a renewed interest in the inculturation of the gospel along with a preferential option for the poor. Some would argue that in recent times, Church leaders have been much less vocal on inculturation and the poor.

As this historical overview has demonstrated, the Mexican people are a people rooted in tradition and change is not easily accepted. Their Catholicism is arguably the most loyal and resistant of any in the world today. Rooted in pre-Christian indigenous fervor, its early evangelizers creatively helped to create a Mexican form of Catholicism. Beset with Church-state tensions throughout its history, it has had a record of defending the poor and oppressed as well as being part of the oppressive structures. As the following chapters demonstrate, once the focus shifts to Mexicans in the United States of America, appreciation of this bittersweet history not only provides a form of social analysis in hindsight, but also examples of what happens when the social and political structures are, once again, radically altered.

Chapter 2

LIVING BETWEEN
TWO WORLDS

A SUMMARY OF THE HISTORY OF MEXICAN-AMERICANS AND THEIR PRESENT REALITY

No soy de aqui, ni soy de allá.
(I'm neither from here, nor from there.)[1]

In the 1997 movie *Selena,* the tragic story of a young *Tejana* singer gunned down at the age of twenty-three, there is a telling scene that illustrates the feeling of placelessness felt by many Mexican-Americans, the frustration of always having to navigate identity. As her father, Abraham Quintanilla, drives the family bus, he shares his wisdom (and aggravation!) with his children, Selena and Abraham, Jr.:

> **Father:** "Being Mexican American is tough. Anglos jump all over you if you don't speak English perfectly. Mexicans jump all over you if you don't speak Spanish perfectly. We got to be twice as perfect as anybody else!...Our family has been here for centuries. And yet they treat us as if we just swam across the Rio Grande. I mean we got to

know about John Wayne and Pedro Infante. We got to know about Frank Sinatra and Agustín Lara. We got to know about Oprah and Cristina! Anglo food is too bland and yet when we go to Mexico we get the runs! That, to me, is embarrassing. Japanese Americans, Italian Americans, German Americans: their homeland is on the other side of the ocean. Ours is right next door…And we have to prove to the Mexicans how Mexican we are. We got to prove to the Americans how American we are. We got to be more Mexican than the Mexicans and more American than the Americans. Both at the same time! It's exhausting! Damn! Nobody knows how tough it is to be a Mexican American!

Selena: "Well Dad, you know it's a good thing we have frijoles and tortillas to keep up our strength for the job…and Menudo."[2]

The previous chapter introduced thirty centuries of Mexican history. This chapter covers much less chronologically, merely a few centuries. Given that the vast territory we delineate today as the U.S. Southwest until 1848 comprised approximately half of the Mexican national soil, much of what was said in the previous chapter remains relevant. Given the space limitations of this book, however, it is important to shift the focus now to the United States of America, both to emphasize the interrelatedness of the two countries and to recognize that the descendents of these Mexican inhabitants of the Southwest, as well as the children of immigrants, are now living in growing proportions throughout all fifty states.[3] In order to describe current realities of the

Mexican-American, this chapter draws extensively from historical and sociological sources.[4]

As much as I would like to incorporate into this story the historic presence of the Native Americans who had lived for untold centuries in these lands conquered by Spain, I am prevented from doing so because of constraints on the book's length. Thus, my focus will be solely on the history of Mexican-Americans. It is laudable to see that current historians, such as Manual G. González, are providing much needed background material on the indigenous peoples as well as their Spanish conquerors in order to understand the political and cultural contours of the present Southwest. In the same vein, González succeeds like few others in demonstrating the ongoing interconnectedness of Mexico and the United States of America.[5]

Some Historical Considerations

The Pre-U.S. Period in the Southwest

As is the case with any territory that has undergone innumerable political changes over the centuries, it is difficult to narrate here the entire history of Mexican-Americans. Thus, only a few salient points will be highlighted. As previously mentioned, the presence of a significant number of Spaniards in the Americas began with the arrival of Christopher Columbus in 1492. Spanish settlements were soon established in the Caribbean and explorers were sent out to the neighboring islands and the mainland, which is now the United States of America. After the conquest of the numerous Indian civilizations in Mexico in the first part of the sixteenth century and others soon after elsewhere in the Americas, the process of evangelizing the Native Americans began. The main vehicle for evangelization in the Southwestern United States of

America and northern Mexico was the mission, or the *reducciones,* as they were sometimes called.[6]

The National Pastoral Plan for Hispanic Ministry,[7] summarizing this work of the religious orders, describes the decades that followed:

> In the 17th century Franciscan missionaries raised elegant churches in the Pueblo towns of New Mexico; Jesuits along the western slopes of New Spain wove scattered Indian rancherias into efficient social systems that raised the standard of living in arid America. But the primacy of evangelization as a cornerstone of Spanish royal policy was swept away by political ambitions in the 18th century; the missions fell victim to secularism. First, the Jesuits were exiled and the order suppressed; Franciscans and Dominicans tried valiantly to stem the tide of absolutism, but their numbers dwindled rapidly and the Church's service to the poor crumbled.[8]

To further complicate matters, this large area, which went from belonging to Spain to being part of the newly established independent country of Mexico in 1820, ended up as part of the territory that the United States of America acquired with the Treaty of Guadalupe Hidalgo in 1848. This pact ended the Mexican-American War, and as a result, Mexico lost half its territory.

In many ways, this takeover by the United States of America was disastrous for the native Hispanic population. Within a matter of years, many families who had lived in these territories for centuries lost their lands and native leadership as a new Anglo-American legal system engulfed them.[9] A traditional community that had known no separation of church and state, for example, now found itself in a very different situation. Through years of long isolation, Spanish folk tradition had become fixed. Espinoza describes New Mexican life in the seventeenth century:

> The history of Spanish culture in New Mexico during the eighteenth century was not very different from that of the seventeenth. The social and religious activities continued as before. Always, it must be emphasized, New Mexico was an isolated frontier community, its people living simple village and rural life. Aside from labors in town and countryside, there were the Church festivals, Masses, marriages, baptisms, and military parades and exercises. The colonists often assembled publicly and privately in dances, prayers, penitential processions, *velorios* for the dead, and burials. During betrothal, marriage, and baptismal celebrations there was feasting, drinking, dancing, and singing of popular songs and ballads.[10]

In his book, *Occupied America: A History of Chicanos,* Rodolfo Acuña has entitled his chapter on the U.S. takeover of New Mexico as "Freedom in a Cage: The Colonization of New Mexico."[11] This title describes vividly the situation of Hispanics in the Southwest during the second half of the nineteenth century. Virgil Elizondo, considered by many to be the father of U.S. Hispanic theology, notes emphatically that the Hispanic of the Southwest is an "exile who never left home."[12] Among the biggest disillusionments for the Hispanics during this era was the lack of support from the Roman Catholic Church.

Incorporation into the United States of America

It was not long after the War of 1848 that the U.S. Catholic hierarchy was given charge of the lands that today encompass the southwestern part of the United States of America. Since the country was still considered mission territory, prelates were brought in from Europe to serve these areas. Except in the case of San Antonio and Dallas, all the first bishops in the dioceses in New Mexico, Arizona, Colorado, and Texas were Frenchmen.[13] Fray Angelico Chavez, OFM, notes a certain irony in the fact that these prelates were Frenchmen, "given that the native priests, having been educated in Durango during the revolutions for independence, were very Mexican. There was a French invasion and they were very anti-French. Then the one sent to them was a Frenchman!"[14] Moises Sandoval criticizes the behavior of some of these "foreign shepherds":

> These bishops, all but one born in Europe, attempted to create a church like the one they had left. The one who perhaps tried the hardest was Jean Baptiste Lamy, the first bishop of New Mexico. He boasted that he was creating a little Auvergne, the name of his province in France. Even the architectural style of the cathedral he started in Santa Fe was French, as were the artisans he brought in to build it.[15]

Sandoval, a layperson originally from New Mexico, is particularly critical of the lack of respect given to the indigenous Church there.

> Lamy and his associate, Joseph P. Machebeuf, later the first bishop of Denver, have been credited for bringing Gallic discipline to the church in New

Mexico. But he also caused division that took generations to reconcile. The Council of Baltimore had appointed Lamy to head the Vicariate of New Mexico *in partibus infidelium* (in the region of the infidels), a fixed phrase for any missionary territory. The designation was perhaps justified in Texas, considering how many indigenous peoples were not yet converted. But it was clearly an affront to the Catholicism that had existed in New Mexico for 250 years. The biased view of the American church and of the bishops sent to the Southwest was that there had been a glorious period of evangelization by the missionaries from Spain and an almost total collapse of the church during the Mexican period. Perhaps that explains why Lamy's relations with the native clergy were poor.[16]

Sandoval looks at the situations of the Hispanic Catholics in Texas and California and reaches the same conclusion: the Hispanic Church had lost its native leaders.[17] With the tremendous influx of non-Hispanics into these territories, particularly after Texas was granted statehood and gold was discovered in California, Hispanics found themselves more and more on the fringe of not only the society in general but also that of the Church.

By the end of the nineteenth century, Hispanic Americans in the Southwest had no institutional voice in the church. The native Hispanic priests who had been their spokesmen in mid-century had all been purged or died out. The removal of the activists had been a powerful lesson for those aging priests who remained. They had realized that they could remain only on condition that they were submissive. They had faded away quietly.[18]

The New Mexican writer sees this loss of native leadership as one of the main reasons the Hispanic laypeople went their own way. "For almost 300 years in New Mexico, 200 years in Texas, and 100 years in California, they relied, of necessity, on their own homespun religious traditions. These served them well."[19]

During the second half of the nineteenth century, non-Hispanic immigrants to the Southwest soon outnumbered the native Hispanic population. As a new system, complete with an entirely different language and court system took effect, Hispanics found themselves pushed aside, often losing their land and, consequently, their political clout.

There was some migration north from Mexico in the years that followed, but these migrations did not become more numerous until the twentieth century. Many immigrants came to the United States of America during the time of the Mexican Revolution in the first decades of the twentieth century.[20]

Immigrant Church in a Protestant Country

Up to this point, what had been the situation of the Catholic Church in the United States of America? Church historian Thomas Bokenkotter distinguishes between the situation in the various territories that would eventually become part of the country and that of the thirteen English colonies. A brief history of the growth of the Church in the Spanish and Mexican South and Southwest has already been given. Mention is now made of the implantation of the Church in the huge French area toward the north of the country. Bokenkotter writes:

Northward lay the huge French area, which also drew many Catholic missionaries, Jesuit, Capuchin, Recollect, and others. The Jesuit Pere Jacques Marquette, discoverer of the Mississippi, and the Jesuit martyrs Isaac Jogues, Jean de Brébeuf, and their companions were among the many who ministered to the spiritual and temporal needs of the Hurons and other Indian tribes. The missionaries also helped establish French Catholic outposts on the Great Lakes and down through the Ohio and Mississippi valleys, a chapter in Catholic history that is recalled by names like Detroit, St. Louis, Vincennes, Louisville, and Marietta.[21]

In reference to the thirteen English colonies, the historian writes about the gradual restriction of religious freedom for Catholics that took hold with the dawning of Protestant political hegemony. With the American Revolution, many of these restrictions were lifted and both Maryland and Pennsylvania passed religious freedom laws in 1776.[22]

Notwithstanding the difficulties met by the Hispanic Church in the Southwest in the nineteenth century, other missionary endeavors in the country met with great success.

No missionary territory in the nineteenth century registered more sensational gains than the Catholic Church in the United States. Thanks to a massive influx of Catholic immigrants—Irish, German, Italians, Poles, and others—the growth of the Catholic Church far outstripped the nation's growth. The American bishops were able to successfully integrate these heterogeneous, polyglot newcomers into the Church structure and provide a huge network of schools, hospitals, and other institutions for them that were soon the envy of the entire Catholic world.[23]

In a relatively short period of time, the Catholic population, complete with all its diversity, grew beyond any foreseeable trend. Bokenkotter details this surge:

> This flood began in the 1820s, with the first wave of Irish immigrants. Largely because of Irish immigrants, the number of Catholics jumped from about 500,000 (out of a U.S. population of 12 million) in 1830 to 3,103,000 in 1860 (out of a U.S. population of 31.5 million)—an increase of over 800 percent—with the number of priests and the number of churches increasing proportionately. So large was this increase that by 1850 Roman Catholicism, which at the birth of the nation was nearly invisible in terms of numbers, had now become the country's largest religious denomination.[24]

This tide of European immigration continued well into the latter part of the nineteenth century. German and Italian mass migrations soon joined those of the Irish:

> The next era, 1860 to 1890, was equally impressive, as the growth of the Church far outstripped the growth of the national population, the Church tripling in size while the nation was only doubling. By 1890 Catholics numbered 8,909,000 out of the nation's 62,947,000. German Catholics, who were previously far less in number, now began nearly to equal the number of Irish immigrants. The wave of immigration, lasting from 1890 to the immigration laws of the 1920s, brought a preponderance

of Italians and eastern Europeans. Over a million Italians alone came during the two decades from 1890 to 1910.[25]

As stated above, the U.S. Church responded admirably to these waves of immigrants. True, controversies such as those regarding the level to which the Church should function as an "Americanizer" abounded. The fact remains, however, that through its parishes, which provided some type of refuge within a new hostile environment, and its schools, which prepared a new generation for life in the United States of America, the Church became the defender of those who had come to America seeking a better life.

As these immigrants moved up the social ladder, so did the Church. Bokenkotter concludes his chapter on the American Church with an observation that by the middle of the twentieth century, it, too, had found a home in the United States of America:

> By the 1950s it was quite obvious to most observers that the Catholic Church in the United States had became a thoroughly American institution. The era of Protestant domination was over. The political significance of this fact was underscored when John F. Kennedy was elected the first Catholic President of the United States, an event that coupled with the reign of Pope John and the calling of his council definitely marked the beginning of a new era in the history of American Catholicism.[26]

Before saying a word about new waves of Mexican migration and that of other Latin Americans, which continue to this day, a few observations about the differences between earlier European and Mexican immigration are in order.[27] These differences do not contradict certain similarities. For example, in the Mexican migration into the Midwest that took place from approximately 1900 to 1930, the Mexican *contratista*, like the Italian *padrone* or the Irish politician before him, served as a liaison with the U.S. community. The village economies of these European immigrants had also been disrupted by impinging capitalism in their home countries. They, too, found themselves struggling to survive in a new country and relied heavily on their family and mutual aid societies to get them through. There are some differences, however, which must be stated.

For one, most of the European immigrants came to the United States of America with the mentality that they would stay permanently.[28] Separated from their native countries by an ocean, it was very unlikely that they would be going back and forth. The Mexicans, on the other hand, were much closer to their native country, and when they were ill-treated in the United States of America, they could more easily return to Mexico, which was a lot closer than Europe. Also, laws against Mexican immigration were few in number and often not enforced. Therefore, Mexicans crossed back and forth between the two countries frequently, often seasonally.

According to González, geography also played a role. European immigrants such as the Germans usually landed in the Eastern cities, which were more industrialized, then often moving to the Midwest. There, despite low wages and monotonous jobs, they were able to find stable work, which allowed for the flourishing of urban ethnic ghettos, which not only provided mutual support and identity but also allowed their children to get an education and their workers to organize. The difference with the Mexicans was that they ended up more often in less industrialized areas and found themselves working in such industries as farming, mining, railroad maintenance and repair, and other similar jobs that often demanded that they frequently migrate. They not only were not able to organize as workers, but low-paying jobs denied them the resources they needed to purchase land, an inability that had serious social and political consequences.

Not to be overlooked is the difference in legal documentation. The Europeans were overwhelmingly legal immigrants, while the Mexicans were not. González cites some important figures to document the difference:

> They [European immigrants] arrived at government reception centers—the most famous being Ellis Island in New York Harbor, established in 1892, which saw 12 million immigrants pass through its waiting rooms—and after a lengthy certification process, only those eligible for entry were admitted. Mexican immigration was largely unregulated. Most immigrants from the south entered the country without their papers—Devra Weber estimates the figure to be as high as 80 percent among migrant workers at the time—a status which was not a problem through the 1920s (except for the 1921–1922 economic slump), a decade when severe labor shortages required the importation of cheap Mexican labor. Beginning in 1929, however, when federal legislation made it a felony to enter the United States illegally, their pattern of irregular entry created many difficulties for *indocumentados* (unauthorized immigrants).[29]

Besides official documentation, another major difference was race. European immigrants were considered to be white while Mexicans were not. For a country where race has often been an explosive topic, this fact is not a minor detail, especially in light of the often held prejudice that whites are superior to nonwhites. Other factors that led to the rise of anti-Mexican feelings were historical. González explains:

> The intensity of anti-Mexican sentiments among Americans had much to do, too, with the unique relationship that had been forged historically between the United States and Mexico. Having enticed Mexico into a major war through a Machiavellian policy and having forcefully divested Mexicans of half their territory, Americans found justification for their aggression by blaming the victims. Moreover, the economic penetration of American capitalism into Mexico during the Porfiriato, based as it was on the exploitation of cheap native labor, fortified the widespread belief that Mexicans were meant to be subservient to whites. Unlike their European counterparts, Mexicans entering the United States found themselves marginalized from the very outset.[30]

González concludes that the end results of these differences, coupled with the fact that the large Mexican migrations took place several decades after the European ones, are that while "the Irish, Italians, and Jews have been absorbed into the middle class, Mexicans, at least three-quarters of them, continue to be predominantly working class people."[31]

A New Wave of Hispanic Migration

In addition to the European immigrants, large numbers of people from Spanish-speaking countries migrated to the United States of America during the end of the nineteenth and throughout the twentieth centuries. Among this large group were those fleeing the political instability caused by the Mexican Revolution, which broke out in 1920. The passage of certain U.S. quota laws that curtailed European immigration, in addition, created a demand for labor during the first part of the century. Mexicans were recruited to fill this gap. In the years that followed, many came as contract laborers, and were forced to return to Mexico when their work was accomplished. Some entered the country illegally and stayed for a time or permanently.[32] Once their children were born in the United States of America (birth in national territory entitles a person to U.S. citizenship), it was easier to obtain legal permission to stay.

The stories of other migrations of Hispanics, either within the country or from outside it, are similar. As some Mexican-Americans went westward or northward seeking employment after World War II, waves of Puerto Ricans and Cubans arrived on the mainland. Puerto Ricans immigrated because of massive job losses in the agricultural sector and other reasons. From 1940 to 1970, the number of farm jobs dropped from 230,000 to 74,000.[33] More than 875,000 Cubans have immigrated to the United States of America during the rule of Fidel Castro following the Cuban Revolution in 1959. According to the 2005 American Community Survey from the U.S. Census Bureau, more than 1.4 million Hispanics (61.4 percent of the total population) live in Miami/Dade County, Florida, their numbers nearly doubling in twenty-five years.[34] Within the last thirty years, Central Americans, particularly Nicaraguans, Salvadorans, and Guatemalans, have migrated to the United States of America in significant numbers. Like others before them, these immigrants have been motivated by political unrest, death threats, and severe poverty in their native countries.[35]

The Present "Signs of the Times"

The Current Socioeconomic Situation of U.S. Hispanics

The previous short summary of the history of Mexicans in the United States of America provides a useful backdrop for understanding the current situation of these people. The fact remains that great social progress for Mexicans in the United States of America has been long in coming. The same can be said for the larger group of Hispanic peoples in this country, mostly descendents of the first European group to set foot in the Americas and the indigenous people they conquered. For the sake of this analysis, given that much demographic data is often presented in this larger aggregate, the Hispanic or Latino population will be described as a whole. Where applicable, certain numbers referring specifically to the U.S. Mexican population are given. An initial bird's-eye view of the Hispanic socioeconomic situation precedes a discussion of the role of the Church in light of this Hispanic sociological reality.

First, a few statistics from the 2000 U.S. Census and subsequent Bureau surveys add some clarity to the Hispanic reality.[36] In 2002, for example, more than one in eight persons in the United States of America was of Hispanic or Latino origin (i.e., 37.4 million Latinos, or 13.3 percent of the total U.S. population). By 2005 the Hispanic population had grown to 14.5 percent of the total population. This figure, of course, does not include persons in institutionalized settings, such as nursing homes or prisons, or may not include those who are undocumented. What ethnic clusters come under this name of *Latino* or *Hispanic*? Even though the largest group are the Mexicans (at 66.9 percent of the total), there are also people from nineteen different Latin American republics, Puerto Rico, and Spain. Central and

South Americans constitute the second largest group at 14.3 percent, with the Puerto Ricans comprising the third largest group at 8.6 percent. Cubans are fourth, with 3.7 percent, and other Hispanics or Latinos number 6.5 percent.[37] The key point here is the tremendous amount of diversity that characterizes this population.[38] Similarly, one must not overlook the fact that the Hispanic population in the United States has grown phenomenally during recent decades ("The Hispanic population increased by 57.9 percent, from 22.4 million in 1990 to 35.5 million in 2000, compared with an increase of 13.2 percent for the total U.S. population... Mexicans increased by 52.9 percent, from 13.5 million to 20.6 million").[39]

This is an impressively young population. In 2002, 34.4 percent of Hispanics were under 18 years of age, compared with 22.8 percent of non-Hispanic whites. Within the Hispanic category, the youngest group are the Mexicans (37.1 percent being under the age of 18) while the oldest group are the Cubans (19.6 percent being under the age of 18).[40] Similarly, the Bureau reported that, while the mean age for the entire country was 35.3 years, for Hispanics it was 25.9 years, a difference of almost 9.5 years. Among that group, the Mexican median age was even younger (24.2 years).[41] The Hispanic population in general, therefore, is extremely young and will continue to increase significantly since so many of the women are of child-bearing age. In addition, most of this population is comprised of persons who were not born in the United States of America. Two in 5 Hispanics (40.2 percent in 2002), for example, were foreign-born.[42] It is essential, therefore, that these two facts about the Latino population—its youth and the large portion of recent arrivals—not be overlooked by pastoral planners!

Latinos also live in family households that tend to be larger than those of non-Hispanic whites. "In 2002, 26.5

percent of family households in which a Hispanic person was the householder consisted of five or more people. In contrast, only 10.8 percent of non-Hispanic White family households were this large. Among Hispanic family households, Mexican family households were most likely to have five or more people (30.8 percent)."[43]

The greatest numbers of Hispanics live in the southwestern part of the United States of America. The state with the largest concentration is California, which has 31.1 percent of the total U.S. Hispanic population. The next largest is Texas, with 18.9 percent.[44] Given the brief history of the Southwest, along with migration trends, this concentration comes as no surprise. Yet, as mentioned at the beginning of this chapter, current demographic trends show that the Latino population has increasingly spread throughout the country, particularly in states that were not traditionally Hispanic.

A lack of education and professional training is a serious problem that contributes to high unemployment. In 2002, more than two in five Hispanics age twenty-five and older had not graduated from high school. That is, there was a 57 percent graduation rate compared with that of non-Hispanic whites, which was 88.7 percent. The level of college education for that same year was also significantly lower, 11.1 percent for Hispanics compared with 29.4 percent for non-Hispanic whites.[45] Edmundo Rodríguez, a Mexican-American pastor of the Jesuit parish in one of the poorest neighborhoods of San Antonio, Texas, had this to say about why so many young Hispanics drop out of school:

> In general, the reasons are economic, cultural, and structural. Economic in that many families cannot even afford to buy their children school clothes. Cultural in that Hispanic students are caught in a

cultural crossfire, living with Hispanic culture at home while feeling pressured at school and work to assimilate and forsake their heritage. Structural in that the school systems are generally not equipped to deal with Hispanics.[46]

His reasons for Hispanics' overrepresentation in the prison population are also linked to social structures.

Like Blacks, Hispanics constitute a disproportionately high percentage of the prison population in states with heavy Hispanic populations. The high rate of dropouts from schools, discouragement and frustration at not being able to get jobs, and lack of opportunities for those who have already been in prison, help enlarge the Hispanic population. The case of the devastating prison riot in New Mexico in 1979 shows how violently that frustration can explode.[47]

As one might expect, a large portion of Hispanics, roughly one-fifth (21.4 percent), lived below the poverty level in 2002. Their poverty rate was more than 2.5 times as high as that for non-Hispanics (7.8 percent). In addition, the Census Bureau reports that "Hispanic children younger than 18 years of age were much more likely than non-Hispanic White children to be living in poverty (28.0 percent compared with 9.5 percent, respectively). Hispanic children represented 17.7 percent of all children in the United States but constituted 30.4 percent of all children in poverty."[48] Such a high number of children living in poverty in a land of abundance seems to characterize recent national trends. A study by the United Nations Children's Fund, for example, found that children in the United States of America are more likely to live in poverty than children in any other industrialized nation. The same report ranked the murder rate for young people in the United States of America as being the highest in the industrialized world.[49]

Judging from the poverty figures quoted above, it is not surprising that Hispanics in general have a significantly lower income than the rest of the population taken together. "Among full-time, year round workers in 2002, 26.3 percent of Hispanics and 53.8 percent of non-Hispanic Whites earned $35,000 or more. Among Latino, full-time, year-round workers, Mexicans had the lowest proportion earning $35,000 or more [23.6 percent]."[50]

Given that data, what is the socioeconomic state of the Latino population in the United States of America? In general, it is a young, working-class population that is much poorer and less well educated than the rest of the nation. It is also characterized by larger families, a good number of which include members of the extended family such as a grandparent. Another important quality is its diversity in terms of the various subgroups that all come under the "Hispanic" or "Latino" umbrella along with the variety of assimilation into U.S. culture that shows itself across generational lines.

Does the fact that Latinos, particularly Mexicans, are generally poorer and less well educated than the general population therefore mean that their culture can be best understood in light of what some have described as "the culture of poverty" or the "urban underclass model"? This theory, whose proponents include such writers as Oscar Lewis, Nicholas Lehmann, and Lawrence Mead, basically holds that a poor person, as a member of the underclass, is, for example, either a social deviant or has low morals, suffers from laziness, apathy, and the like, and tends to experience much social alienation.[51] Up until recently, this notion went virtually unchallenged.

This high level of poverty, however, does not necessarily mean that the Latino's quality of life is inevitably lower. In a fascinating study of Latinos in California directed by medical sociologist David E. Hayes-Bautista, this team of researchers presented substantial evidence to challenge many of the myths perpetuated about the Latino in California. Their conclusions show that, contrary to popular perception and even previous sociological studies, the Latino does not fit into the "underclass and cultural deficit paradigms" that often characterize poor populations in this country.

For example, despite their poverty, Latinos have high levels of labor force participation. In terms of education, there are significant signs of progress if generational differences are observed. The researchers did not find a sense of alienation or loss of identity in terms of mainstream culture as some social scientists have posited in the past. Among the most positive traits they uncovered besides the previously mentioned high labor force participation were strong family formation, good health indicators, and low welfare utilization. The researchers state the crux of their argument in these words:

> There is an apparent contradiction in this situation: a group with the highest poverty and lowest education rates demonstrates some of the most markedly positive behavior regarding family, work, health and the community. Under most current assumptions about the way minority groups are assumed to behave, this should not be the case.[52]

There are those who question Hayes-Bautista's findings, accusing him of being "overzealous in accentuating the positive, in the process obscuring real family problems and creating a mythology of their own."[53] The jury is still out on these sociological trends.

Another study done with Latina garment workers in El Paso, Texas, from 1992 to 1994 reached the same conclusion as Hayes-Bautista et. al. The researcher, Juanita García Fernández, describes the results of her study, whose purpose was to examine the Latinas' workplace (small, medium, and large clothing factories), community, and personal and home issues "in order to quantify the necessities and progress needed for the garment worker population."[54]

> The survey shows that these women demonstrate middle class attitudes and behavior toward the basic institutions in our society, especially family, work, and education. The women demonstrate[d] …high labor participation, low welfare and government assistance dependency, strong health indicators, awareness of the need of education, strong family unity. These characteristics…demonstrate that Latino garment workers do not comply with the expected profile of the UUM [urban underclass model]. Although the population in the study did have low levels of education and a high poverty level, it is wrong to assume from these facts alone that they conform to the UUM.[55]

Elsewhere, she concludes that one of the major reasons for their poverty is simply that they "work in the garment industry which offers low-paying, dead-end jobs that give little opportunity for occupational mobility and advancement."[56]

While the work of these researchers is still at a pioneering stage, they definitely represent a challenge to the urban underclass model. From a sociological standpoint, then, what is the factor that accounts for the resiliency of U.S. Latinos? Again, their theologians are now beginning to explore an inherent world of meaning—a spirituality, one might say— which provides an unmistakable source of strength. In regards to Mexicans, the topic of the resiliency of their spirituality or the relevance of their emerging theology is specifically taken up in subsequent chapters. For now, a look at Latinos in general in relation to the institutional Church helps to round out this background view.

The Role of the Church

According to a sociological study done in 1985 by Roberto Gonzalez and Michael LaVelle, 83 percent of the Hispanic Catholics sampled considered religion important, yet 88 percent are not active in their parishes.[57] Nevertheless, the study also found that Hispanics have high levels of adherence to orthodox Catholic beliefs, and that they engage in many folk religious practices, some of Marian inspiration. The study also found that a higher percentage of Hispanic Catholics appear to attend Mass on Sundays and holy days of obligation than is generally accounted for by conventional pastoral wisdom.[58]

To what extent has the Church been present and actively involved in the service of the Hispanic community in the United States of America over the decades? Several writers on this subject say that the Church's record for being in solidarity with this marginal population is mixed. Among the critics is Moises Sandoval, the editor of *Maryknoll*, the monthly magazine of the Catholic Foreign Mission Society of America, as well as its bilingual counterpart, *Revista Maryknoll*. Extensive use of his history of the Hispanic Church in the United States of America entitled *On the Move* has already been made.[59]

In an article published prior to this account, he traces the history of the campesino and the Catholic Church in the Southwestern United States of America.[60] His overall conclusion is that the Church, aside from its influential intervention in the farm labor negotiations of the late 1960s and early 1970s, has consistently taken a more conservative position in respect to social change. A brief history of the Church in the Southwest since the arrival of the first evangelizers in the sixteenth century reveals a Church beset with the problem of having too few resources to tend to its Hispanic flock. Even as late as the nineteenth century, the Church hierarchy viewed the Hispanic as the object of evangelization, never the subject.

Sandoval concludes that the Church, instead of making a radical option for the poor today *(accompañamiento)*, has chosen to offer some relief aid *(caridad)* and devote the majority of its resources to the middle class, its biggest financial backer. Sandoval reminds us of the need to look back to history for social analysis. True, the Church lacked resources but part of that dearth was caused by its failure to inculturate (as evidenced by its imported clergy over the last four centuries there).[61]

Leveling similar charges that the Church has failed to fully inculturate within the culture of U.S. Hispanics, Yolanda Tarango, a Mexican-American woman religious, brings home the point that while the Church has reached "the ends of the earth" geographically, it is still struggling to be universal.[62] Tracing the emergence of the Mexican-American historically and culturally in the Southwest, she criticizes the American Catholic Church, especially in Texas, for promoting "Americanization" along with evangelization.

She believes that the lingering feeling of Mexican-Americans toward the official Church is that it is an Anglo institution. Such alienation has, consequently, transferred religious practices to the home. The system of evangelization in which most Hispanics have been evangelized, therefore, is a circular one whose religion is taught through feeling and example. On the other hand, the official Church's method is linear and individualistic. Hispanics are still viewed as objects of mission and the emphasis remains on assimilation.

A New Exodus

Discontent with the Church has led some Hispanics to gravitate toward Protestant groups.[63] True, Protestantism, as Justo González notes, had existed for some time in Latin America, but the fact remains that the Catholic Church has lost and is continuing to lose much of its flock. González describes some of the historical appeal of Protestantism to U.S. Hispanics.

But not all Protestant Hispanics in the United States entered the country as Protestants. Many were converted in the United States, through processes similar to those that took place in Latin America. In the nineteenth century, Protestantism appeared to be as the vanguard of progress, while Roman Catholicism, especially under Pius IX, was going through its most authoritarian and reactionary period. After the Mexican-American War, the Roman Catholic hierarchy in the conquered territories was in the hands of the invaders, and generally in their service. Actually, the first Mexican-American bishop was not named until well into the second half of the twentieth century. These circumstances gave rise to anticlerical feelings similar to those which appeared in Latin America at the time of independence. And this in turn opened the way for Protestantism.[64]

Thus, during the nineteenth century, many perceived the Catholic Church as backward and anti-Hispanic while Protestants were seen as progressive.

Today the trend to abandon the Roman Church has only escalated. As the saying goes, "people vote with their feet." There are some who feel that these non-Catholic groups have done a much better job of catering to Hispanics and immigrants in general than has the Catholic Church. Allan Deck, one of the foremost experts in the field, stresses that since there is not a single cause for this mass exodus, there is not a single remedy. In an article that appeared in 1985, he offers numerous reasons and suggests various possible solutions.[65]

He discusses the results of several meetings that attempted to deal with this flight of Hispanic Catholics. The single most prominent aspect that emerged from the dialogue of bishops in Alta and Baja California was the need for more personalism in all dealings with Hispanic people. The Church has often failed to inculturate, often being too territorial and coming across as lacking in focus.[66]

The fundamentalists, on the other hand, "offer the Hispanic an attractive, coherent package." Fixed doctrines, simple or even simplistic morality, and emotionally charged worship make fundamentalism very attractive to a Hispanic largely ignored by his or her native Church. The article's greatest merit is its challenge to the Catholic Church to open its eyes. The fundamentalists are making inroads with Hispanics because they have made more of an effort to inculturate into a less cerebral milieu.

Edmundo Rodríguez, the Jesuit pastor previously mentioned who later became provincial of the New Orleans Jesuit Province, raises the question from another perspective.

The Protestant and Pentecostal churches are making great inroads into the Hispanic community. They are perceived as churches of the poor and for the poor (whether this be the reality or not); many of them take in chemically dependent people and turn their lives around. Generally, their buildings are much simpler and often these are "storefront" churches; they are basically lay churches in which anyone willing to spend time in training can become an apostle. There is also a perception that the people who belong to these little churches are not afraid to come into people's houses and deal with the worst problems they find there: addictions, violence, and strained relationships between family members. The Catholic Church, on the other hand, is seen as being uncomfortable with poverty and as not dealing with the real problems that poor people generally experience. That, in my opinion, is why the fundamentalist churches are so attractive to poorer Hispanics.[67]

As has been demonstrated, the Church's ministry to Hispanics has been plagued with many difficulties. Among the two most difficult have been how to make, in the words of Puebla, a "preferential option of the poor" and how to inculturate the message of the gospel so as to stem the tide created by the present mass exodus.

A Prophetic Presence

The U.S. bishops addressed the issue of Hispanic ministry with a pastoral letter in 1983 and a pastoral plan in 1987. Although issued by the hierarchy, this work, the *National Pastoral Plan for Hispanic Ministry,* is the culmination of three *encuentros,* or national meetings, held in

1972, 1977, and 1985 to collect input and feedback from the grassroots Hispanic Church.[68] The *encuentro* held in 1985, the Tercer Encuentro, is particularly characterized by consultation, study, and reflection at all levels. It was attended by 1,150 delegates.[69] As the *Pastoral Plan* notes, Hispanics, despite their economic poverty, have much to offer the U.S. Church:

> This same people, due to its great sense of religion, family, and community, are a prophetic presence in the face of materialism and individualism of society. Since the majority of Hispanics are Catholic, their presence can be a source of renewal within the Catholic Church in North America. Because of its youth and growth, this community will continue to be a significant presence in the future.[70]

Other writers add their assessment of the spiritual riches of the Hispanic culture to the bishops' statement. Kenneth G. Davis, a Conventual Franciscan, sees the presence of Hispanics in the Church as a blessing. In them he finds less of a modern, secularistic taint. "It is precisely because Hispanics are Catholic and not part of our dominant society that they are in a unique position to help us distinguish between what is authentically Catholic in our society and what is the trappings of purely civil religion or cultural convention."[71]

In a similar vein, Allan Deck describes some of the differences between the Hispanic and dominant North American culture. His analysis fleshes out the bishops' hope that Hispanics mark a prophetic presence in the Church.

> The North American culture is one closely wrapped in personal development, in individualism, in secularism, while the Hispanic culture

stresses the collective aspects of personal life: the extended family, the interrelatedness of people's spiritual and temporal lives. The Anglo-American world stresses the independence of the individual, while the Hispanics' world is hierarchical and stresses the dependence and interdependence of the individual on the family, the church, and the community. Hispanic culture, with its strong emphasis on the religious aspect of life, feels a definite attraction to a family- and community-based approach to religion. The Hispanic looks for more expressive ways of living his or her faith.[72]

Some theologians have taken a serious look at Hispanic spirituality, of which popular religiosity is an important part, and have begun its systematization. Rosa María Icaza, for example, a Sister of Charity of the Incarnate Word, describes the spirituality of Mexican and Mexican-American Catholics. Her observations probably hold true for Latin American spirituality in general. She concludes that for Hispanics "spirituality is translated into the love of God which moves, strengthens and is manifested in love of neighbor and of self."[73]

She uses numerous examples to prove her point. Drawing greatly from popular religiosity, she describes an incarnational spirituality where symbols and relationships are of utmost importance, whether between the individual and God or between the individual and others. Without polarizing various touchy issues such as feminism or clericalism, she succeeds in showing that both women and priests play an important role within the culture. She concludes with the observation that a Hispanic pastoral theology is still in process.[74]

As the above article by a Hispanic theologian suggests, there is today an emerging U.S. Hispanic theology that is attempting to identify and promote Christian values within

Hispanic culture. Although, in the words of the bishops' pastoral, "no other European culture has been in this country longer than the Hispanic,"[75] it is only recently, with the advent of such Hispanic theologians as Virgil Elizondo, Allan Deck, and María Pilar Aquino, that these voices are being heard in the arena of theological scholarship.[76]

The Academy of Catholic Hispanic Theologians of the United States (ACHTUS) was formed recently and is already serving an important role in the development of this emerging local theology. What is interesting to note about this group of Hispanic theologians is that at least one-quarter are female, a significant number are laypersons, and just about all are actively engaged in a pastoral area.

This last fact helps to guarantee that their reflection is coming out of a pastoral experience. The need for insertion and dialogue is something spoken about in Puebla (#'s 650, 122, and 1307), and is summarized in the term *pastoral de conjunto*. The bishops' letter describes this strategy as "a pastoral focus and approach to action arising from shared reflection among the agents of evangelization."[77]

A Challenge Echoed

Our examination of Hispanic Catholics, particularly Mexicans, in the U.S. Church, has led us through a brief history that revealed both an old and a new presence, a social analysis that rendered the image of a young, generally poor, and uneducated population very much in need of the Church's assistance, yet, as the theological reflection highlighted, a people not without innumerable social and religious gifts. In fact, the evidence for debunking the urban underclass model as it has been applied to Latinos in the United States of America calls for the development of new paradigms, ones that take into account their spirituality, or their world of meaning in relation to the sacred. Religion may very well provide a unifying factor for the tremendously diverse Latino communities.

For these and other reasons, they will continue to play an important role in the U.S. Church. Despite the present exodus of Hispanic Catholics from the Church, it is said that by the year 2010 the majority of Catholics in the United States of America will be Hispanic or of Hispanic origin. It is not the first time that the U.S. Church has been made up of a large immigrant population. The great successes with the waves of poor Europeans who came to America in the second half of the nineteenth and the early part of the twentieth centuries were not obtained without faith, creativity, and adaptation. Through these struggles the Church matured and grew to encompass a great diversity, surely the most diverse, in the world. Parochial schools, seminaries for a native clergy, hospitals, orphanages, and national parishes were a welcome sight for immigrants who had left everything to come to America and form part of a new country and a new Church.[78]

Once again, the Catholic Church in the United States of America has an opportunity to be a Church of the poor, this time the poor already within its dioceses. Will it welcome them and see them as a blessing and not a problem to be solved, as just another ethnic group to be assimilated? The question remains.

While chapter 5 takes a deeper look into the theology that is emerging around the Mexican-American practice of the faith, we now turn to a brief treatment of the spirituality behind that theology, a theology that takes into account both suffering and God's infinite grace. In the words of Paul's Letter to the Hebrews, "For land which has drunk the rain that often falls upon it, and brings forth vegetation useful to those for whose sake it is cultivated, receives a blessing from God" (Heb 6:7).

Chapter 3

"LA VIDA ES SAGRADA"

MEXICAN SPIRITUALITY

No hay mal que por bien no venga.
(Every dark cloud has a silver lining.)

The word *spirituality* is very much in the air today. A simple browse through a bookstore reveals an abundance of volumes on this topic. Likewise, workshops and retreats that include this word in their title often attract large crowds. The phrase "I am spiritual but not religious" has become quite popular, if somewhat vacuous. Some writers wonder if this concern for spirituality is not a reaction to what has been an overreliance on science and consumerism, or perhaps a reaction to what some have perceived as religion's attempt to limit or define the sacred. While there are many meanings now associated with the term *spirituality,* the one employed here is captured by the phrase "walking in the Spirit." Because the focus is not just on that which is not material, it includes all aspects of the human person. That is why the phrase, *"La vida es sagrada"* (Life is sacred), sums up this holistic understanding. Spirituality understood in this manner is the way we consciously choose to involve ourselves, or "be swept up by" that which we consider most important in our lives. St. Paul first uses the term when speaking about "spiritual persons" in his First Letter to the Corinthians (2:13, 15).[1]

In the case of Mexican and Mexican-American Christians, as is true for many others, the spiritual quest is not one made alone. As part of a traditional culture in which the sacred and the profane are not as separated as in most modern cultures, one cannot speak about Mexican culture without mentioning religion or spirituality. The murals found in barrios in many large U.S. cities are often filled with religious symbols such as that of pre-Christian Aztec deities, Our Lady of Guadalupe, Jesus, saints, and angels. These figures rarely appear in isolation; often they depict a relationship with a people who continue to struggle for justice, as in the case of the United Farm Workers. Although Mexican spirituality is unique in many ways, it has some characteristics in common with more encompassing Hispanic spirituality.[2] This spirituality reflects not only centuries of lived Christianity in Latin America but also a new synthesis, or *mestizaje,* gradually taking shape on U.S. soil. As mentioned above, for example, it is not uncommon to see the image of Our Lady of Guadalupe depicted in contemporary Chicano art.[3] A young Mexican graduate student who had been away for studies in the United States of America visited Our Lady's shrine in Mexico City upon his return. Reflecting on La Virgen's omnipresence in that massive city, in U.S. Mexican neighborhoods, and finally, in his vulnerable heart he wrote,

> Yesterday we went to visit "Lupita" [affectionate name for Our Lady of Guadalupe]. It had been ten years since I had been back to see her. I felt much joy at being there. The shrine is a church built for people, an enormous tent which extends beyond its physical limits, from the walls of a barrio in Chicago to the second class buses in the south of

Mexico. I walk amidst the city and am struck to see her in all places, so close, belonging to everyone, so necessary. I have never been very marian or guadalupan, but this is what happens when you eat too many bagels [i.e., you find yourself away from your native habitat], but I am living a time in my life when I need to trust in God a great deal, and, well, la "Lupita" knows a great deal about what that means.[4]

Because she is so much a part of the Mexican psyche, even some Mexican Protestants are now starting to reflect on the meaning of La Virgen for them.[5] More will be said about her later. For now, let us look at some of the characteristics of Mexican spirituality that often appear in pastoral counseling, spiritual direction, or popular religious celebrations.

Complex

Because of the cultural complexity that still exists in Mexico, a land where, according to government figures, sixty-two indigenous languages are still spoken today[6] almost five hundred years since the arrival of the Spanish, a people's way of acting and worshipping in a particular region, such as the northern deserts, will differ greatly from that of the southern, more traditional areas. As someone once said, "There are many Mexicos."[7] Just within Catholicism, throughout cities, towns, and villages, there are innumerable specific devotions to Christ, Mary, and the saints under a wide array of titles. For example, although devotion to Mary, the Mother of God, often takes the form of Our Lady of Guadalupe, there are also other popular regional Marian devotions such as those of Nuestra Señora de San Juan de Los Lagos or Nuestra Señora de Zapopan.

This religious and cultural complexity not only existed in the Americas before the arrival of the Europeans, but was also a result of regional differences that existed in Spain, a peninsula that is a centuries-old blend of Iberian, Basque, Phoenician, Greek, Roman, Visigothic, North African, Moorish, and Jewish cultures. In the case of Mexico, this Spanish intermingling mixed with the indigenous peoples, the result being a new *mestizaje*. In the case of some regions, particularly along the Atlantic coast where African slaves had been brought from across the ocean, a new group, the *mulatos,* a combination of the African and the Spanish, emerged. While this blend, or *mulatez,* is not as common in Mexico as in other Latin American countries, particularly in the Caribbean, it should still be noted and celebrated.

Popular and Communal

One of the things that immigrants from Latin America often find difficult when they come to the United States of America is the lack of communal observance of celebrations. For example, some who are accustomed to not having to work during part or all of Holy Week in their native countries are surprised to discover that in the United States of America they are lucky to get Good Friday off. Some have told me that in these situations, where they can no longer assume that the culture around them is generally Catholic, they find themselves looking for communal celebrations such as those around holy days where they can get in touch with what is important for their culture, such as Jesus, Mary, and the other saints.

Partly because of its sociohistorical emergence in a people not unfamiliar with diversity, conquest, and resistance, Mexican spirituality, like that of the rest of Latin America, is not that of some elite group. In the words of

Allan Figueroa Deck, "it [Hispanic spirituality] does not have its gurus nor does it move in rarefied circles. This spirituality is bound up with the Hispanic Catholic civilization."[8] It is difficult for modern cultures, which give a great deal of importance to the individual, to understand the evangelization of the New World, especially as it relates to conversion. In the words of Deck, "modern European and North American cultures have tended to conceive of conversion as Protestants do. For many of us, conversion means a personal decision to believe and follow Christ in the church. Conversion, in this view, is fundamentally a personal matter."[9] Contrasting the pre-Tridentine approach used by the sixteenth-century mendicant friars, Deck sees this conversion as a collective, communal event, time and circumstances not permitting otherwise. In other words, by trying to focus their energies not on individual conversions but on the conversion of communal symbols, rituals, and customs, the missionaries sought to win over the hearts of indigenous peoples to Christ. Evidence of what Deck labels "cultural conversion" is found today in the persistence of a popular religiosity that can only be understood by exploring its symbols, rituals, and cultural myths. Unlike mainstream American Catholicism or mainstream Protestantism, which has "opted to take the route of the cognitive, literate, rational exposition of the faith," Hispanic Catholicism (and Hispanic spirituality by derivation), being rooted in oral language and myth, has "opted for the heart. It seeks to fill the heart first and then, hopefully, the head."[10]

This emphasis on the heart, as articulated in community, is clearly evident in the various successful movements that have taken root in Latino communities, such as Charismatic Renewal, Cursillo, Marriage Encounter, and youth movements that often invite others to experience their Christian faith more vibrantly through an experience of an intense weekend of hearing faith testimonies or sharing their own struggles to follow Christ in the world. They are often very good about providing a supportive community after this passionate experience. The importance of these movements is in their appeal to the emotive and communal aspects of the culture, especially in a situation where the majority of Hispanics are recent immigrants who often feel isolated in their new country. As in the example of Good Friday, which for many now constitutes a working day, it is in walking together the live Via Crucis in their neighborhood that they experience being part of a larger group that walks with Christ and the Blessed Mother, particularly in their most difficult hour.[11]

Another manifestation of this popular and communal aspect of the spirituality of Mexicans, especially recent immigrants, is the tensions that surface within families and among friends when an individual leaves the Catholic Church and joins another religious group, particularly when such events as Christmas, Holy Week, and saints' feast days cannot be celebrated, at least not in the way the family has done for centuries. Similarly, sacramental events such as baptisms, first communions, and weddings, where family members are expected to participate, can also become problematic, especially if the family wishes to include these former Catholics in the liturgical celebrations. For example, according to Church law, parents are to choose good, practicing Catholics as godparents for their children. In a culture where "godparentage," or *compadrazgo,* carries a great deal of meaning and forges new and often deeper relationships between persons, not being able to choose the proper person because he or she has left the Catholic Church can be very problematic. It may also be the case that the former Catholic, now a member of a Protestant denomination that does not believe in infant baptism, may no longer feel comfortable in accepting the responsibility of being a godparent.

Although these difficulties may not seem particularly problematic in the long run, I am struck by a statement I once heard a young woman say about a friend of hers who decided not to ask a very good friend to be the godmother of her child because she had moved in with her boyfriend and was therefore living out of the bonds of holy matrimony. Her remark, "She chose him over us," reveals not only her disappointment but also her commitment to her Church and to her family. The point here is simply that more communal societies will often expect more of their members, even religiously.

Festive

One of the stereotypes of Mexicans is that they are a fun-loving, partying people. Images of mariachis playing their trumpets, people dancing, and great quantities of food, friends, and family all come to mind. My non-Mexican friends who work in parishes frequently question the amount of money that is spent on celebrations that take place around key moments in persons' lives such as welcoming (baptism), coming to the table and growth in the faith and in society (first communion and *quinceañera*), commitment (marriage, religious life, and anniversaries), and even death (funerals). There is a popular Mexican song, "Cielito Lindo," which has the following rousing chorus:

> Ay, yai, yai, yai, canta y no llores.
> Porque cantando se alegran, Cielito Lindo, los
>   corazones.

These lines, dedicated to a beautiful woman who is called "Cielito Lindo" (beautiful heaven or sky), translate as "Sing and don't cry, because it is through song that hearts become joyful." One might have begun to suspect that by festive, I am referring to much more than a party. A patronal fiesta for a saint or a family member, for example, is not just the party that goes with a particular celebration. In the case of an annual feast held on the Virgin's or saint's day, the fiesta includes a procession (which not only invokes the participation of all but also the element of pilgrimage), a Mass or Eucharist (which assembles the community around the Lord's table), and a community meal of some sort afterward that is often accompanied by dancing. Some have summarized these communal celebrations as "Misa, Mesa, Musa."[12]

Despite a history of suffering and oppression, Mexican spirituality is characterized by a life-giving inner strength. As the chorus to "Cielito Lindo" suggests, the culture exhibits a general sunny disposition needed to combat life's difficulties. The large number of family and communal celebrations provide an oasis in a life beset with an infinite number of problems that so often plague a population much poorer than the general one. Likewise, art and music play a key role in this affirmation of life. For the ancient Aztecs, indigenous inhabitants of Mesoamerica, truth was expressed not in rational exposition but in "flor y canto" (flower and song). Is it any wonder, then, that flower and song remain powerful symbols used in worship to this day? No Guadalupe celebration would be complete without them.

The noted Mexican poet Octavio Paz, who garnered a Nobel Prize for literature, goes so far as to label the fiesta an excess. "Wasting money and expending energy affirm the community's wealth in both." He adds:

> The fiesta is by nature sacred, literally or figuratively, and above all it is the advent of the unusual. It is governed by its own special rules, that set it apart from other days, and it has a logic, an ethic

and even an economy that are often in conflict with everyday norms. It all occurs in an enchanted world: time is transformed to a mythical past or a total present; space, the scene of the fiesta, is turned into a gaily decorated world of its own; and the persons taking part cast off all human or social rank and become, for the moment, living images. And everything takes place as if it were not so, as if it were a dream. But whatever happens, our actions have a greater lightness, a different gravity. They take on other meanings and with them we contract new obligations. We throw down our burdens of time and reason.[13]

It is because of this release, this freedom, even if only for a short time, that fiestas are life-giving. Roberto Goizueta describes the fiesta as "life in the subjunctive,"[14] that is, "what if…?" What if we all treated each other in regular life as we try to do around the Eucharistic table? What if we really did eradicate hunger in the world and all had plenty?

The fiesta is not the same as a *pachanga* or *reventón*, which is more of a wild bash. The fiesta is sacred; it celebrates a specific event, unlike the *pachanga*. It not only commemorates an important date such as Christmas, a saint's feast, a birthday or anniversary, or a rite of passage, such as baptism or marriage, but it also calls for certain rituals and organization. Invitation, food preparation, decoration, and music are ways in which the community shares its riches. In the case of a patronal feast in Mexico, this celebration is a convocation of the entire community, rich or poor, each contributing according to her or his means. At least for the time being, all are equal. All can feel part of a larger whole. Maybe later there is scarcity, but in the fiesta there is abundance! It is a way of charging one's batteries for what lies ahead.[15] Any wonder, then, that so many new immigrants try to return to their villages for these yearly celebrations?

The spirit behind the fiesta, encompassing such virtues as hospitality, service, kinship, friendship, and communal riches amid individual poverty, augments and in many ways flows out of the sacred rituals and sacraments often celebrated in key moments in people's lives.[16] Influenced by the traditional Iberian practice of the fiesta consisting of a procession, a Mass, or a Eucharistic celebration, followed by a meal of some sort, the Mexican fiesta is much more than a party or simply a social that happens after a liturgy. It is the same spirit of the goodness of God, nature, and community being celebrated.[17]

Relational

There is a Brazilian song, "Quiero tener un million de amigos" (I want to have a million friends), composed and sung by Roberto Carlos, which became very popular in Mexico in its Spanish form. (Remember, the language of Brazil is Portuguese, *not* Spanish.) This popularity speaks of the importance that the Mexican places on having friends and on relationality. Compared to the U.S. dominant culture, Mexicans generally value belonging over personal achievement. More in sync with traditional societies where the individual derives her or his importance from the group rather than from individual accomplishments, relations take on a singular quality. Family and friends must be consulted when important decisions are made, for their welfare should have priority in the person's life. For example, Mexicans are less likely to put their elderly in nursing homes or to put up children for adoption. Whether aged or young, these persons are the responsibility of the community. It is not uncommon to see immigrants struggling to support their families back home, and often to bring over family members and take care of them until they are able to stand on their own feet. Similarly, hospitality and care for one's own during times of sickness or imprisonment reveal gospel values.

Gahisi Sowande, a black man who had been in prison for almost twenty years, had this to say about the loyalty of family members: "What I notice about the Mexican prisoners is that no matter if they are in prison for a year or 20 years, their family unity is going to close ranks around them and visit them no matter what."[18] This love and support is not seen as something that ends at death but continues long after, as the importance given to funerals and yearly memorial Masses attests. Similarly, el Día de los Muertos (Day of the Dead) celebrations demonstrate a deep sense of the "communion of saints," that is, a strong connection with all those who have gone before them.[19]

Women, particularly in the relational role of mother and grandmother, are often the ones who serve as reconcilers, domestic prayer leaders, storytellers, community leaders, and care providers. They often lead many popular piety rituals such as praying the rosary, seasonal customs such as the Advent practice of *posada* (a novena that reenacts Mary and Joseph's search for lodging), or blessing their children, especially when they are departing on a journey. Social scientist Dean R. Hoge and his research team found that "Latino Catholics, and especially young Latino Catholics, are less involved in parish life than other Catholics, while at the same time they practice more personal and family devotions than others."[20]

In Mexican Catholic spirituality, God is often encountered through Our Lady of Guadalupe and other Marian devotions. More will be said about the Guadalupan devotion below, but for now suffice it to say that from the seventeenth century she has been a powerful symbol of a compassionate

God who is close to people, especially when they are suffering. At a time when the indigenous peoples in Mesoamerica were being told that their culture, as well as their gods, were demonic and a thing of the past, she appears in symbols of compassion, reverence, and belonging that speak to both the conquered and the conqueror. In this way, she is the "Mother of the new creation."[21] A similar phenomenon occurs with the saints, who are seen as friends and powerful intercessors. Again, similar to other traditional societies that engage intermediaries, Hispanic Catholics often honor Mary and the saints because they are related to Christ. If I care about you, I will also care about your mother and your friends and your family. Or, at least, that's the theory!

As in any honest relationship, persons have the confidence to ask for favors. Just as one would not hesitate to ask one's mother or relatives for a favor, intercessory prayers to Mary and the saints for one's loved ones are common, especially if the loved ones are in need of physical or spiritual healing. Miraculous healings are seen as possible if God wills them. There is a saying that goes "Cuando Dios no quiere, ni los santos pueden" (When God does not will something, not even the saints are able to do it).

Given the importance of relationality to Mexican spirituality, what logically follows is that persons are more important than laws.[22] "The sabbath was made for humankind, and not humankind for the sabbath" (Mark 2:27). As the biblical understanding of justice stresses, justice is about fulfilling one's obligations in a covenant relationship. This relational characteristic of Mexican spirituality may manifest itself in the area of social justice. This connection between social justice and spirituality is clearly seen, for example, in Cesar Chávez's incorporation of such popular faith practices as pilgrimage, fasts, prayers, and devotion to Our Lady of Guadalupe into the struggle to organize farm workers.[23] As is the case of the grassroots women leaders mentioned above, the quest for justice cannot be separated from spirituality. As María Pilar Aquino notes, many Latinas live out their spirituality by espousing the cause of the poor and defenseless.

> For Latina women, Christian faith is not a fragmentary aspect of their life or of their own cultural identity. The struggle of these women for a new earth and for new ways of being and living in the church, where they can participate as members of their own right, is inspired by their conviction of faith, and affects their whole life. To state just a few of their activities, many Latina women are committed to human rights groups, to the defense of the undocumented, to solidarity movements, to peace, to ecological, artistic, and cultural movements, to liberating evangelization groups, to the affirmation of indigenous communities, to the defense of civil rights, to the affirmation of women, young people, children, and the aged, and so on. Consequently, theological reflection must take into account their multiple interests as believers, as poor, and as women, together with their religious and cultural values.[24]

Such concern for justice is just another expression of the sacredness of human life, further evidence that "La vida es sagrada" (Life is sacred).

Transcendent

Even though there is great importance given to the human in Mexican spirituality, a characteristic that can partly be traced to the early influence of the Franciscans, Augustinians, Dominicans, and Jesuits who evangelized much of the country and whose spirituality is very connected with the person of Jesus, it nonetheless affirms a transcendent God. Such phrases as "Si Dios es servido" (If God is served by this or that), "Nombre sea de Dios" (In God's name we go forth); "Primeramente Dios" or "Dios mediante" (primarily through the grace of God) speak of a radical dependence on a God who is both near and far. This God, who is almighty (*todopoderoso* or *muy grande* [very great]), took on flesh and became one of us.

Devotions around the human Jesus often catch the eye of the outsider, for example, those surrounding the Christ Child, El Niño Dios. The human reality of the incarnation is brought home by a common Christmas carol that speaks of the Virgin washing diapers in the river ("La Virgen lava pañales"). Similarly, there are devotions to the suffering or dead Christ, El Nazareno (the Nazarene); El Divino Preso (the divine prisoner); El Santo Entierro (the deceased Christ). Mexicans are able to relate to this Jesus who was vulnerable as a little child and endured much suffering in his life.

Yet these images are only part of the story. Images of the Sacred Heart of Jesus, the symbol of the love and mercy of the risen Christ, abound in Mexican homes. For Mexicans and other Latin Americans, therefore, the humanity and transcendence of Christ remain essential to their devotion. In reference to the suffering Christ, Orlando Espín, a Cuban-American theologian, comments, "This dying Jesus, however, is so special because he is not just another human who suffers at the hands of evil humans. He is the divine Christ, and this makes his innocent suffering all the more dramatic...His passion and death express his solidarity with all men and women throughout history who have also innocently suffered at the hands of evildoers."[25]

Having described five traits of Mexican, and consequently Mexican-American spirituality (its complexity, its popularity and communality, its festivity, its relationality, and its transcendence), the following chapter gives further examples of how this spirituality is incorporated into the everyday life of these diverse communities, especially in regards to key devotions and celebrations. It is important to keep in mind that this spirituality is one that is passed on to generations, not in a cerebral manner, but in the time-tested pedagogy of popular religiosity.[26]

Chapter 4

" ¡VIVA LA VIRGEN! "

MEXICAN FEASTS AND CUSTOMS

Cuando Dios amanece, para todos aparece.
(When God rises in the morning, he rises for all.)

Long before educators extolled the importance of participatory learning, traditional communities understood that beliefs and values are best taught through ritual, story, and the corporal works of mercy. A Mexican-American Sister describes the ambience in which she, one of seven children, heard her parents' stories about overcoming adversity.

> Mom and Dad at the kitchen table telling us of the difficult times they had in Mexico—my father pulls an imaginary belt to the last hole, yet they laugh as they recount the lean times. This story is told in the kitchen as Mom turns the expanding flour tortilla on the griddle, the beans are bubbling as they are mashed in black iron skillet, and meat sizzles with a generous portion of onions in another skillet. We all sit around the table taking turns waiting for the next tortilla to drop on the clean washcloth. It will feel the quick stab of a knife, the quick release of its built-up steam, and butter melting as it spreads through its insides as we fold or roll it into our

> hands and mouth. My parents are divorced, yet those common memories hold them laughing wholeheartedly as best of friends. I am puzzled: how could they laugh at hunger?[1]

One cannot help but notice the importance of food at these heart-sharing events. Jesus, in giving us the Eucharist, understood this life-giving context quite well.

This same wisdom of transmitting the Church's beliefs and values through ritual, story, and charitable works is now part of any good parish confirmation preparation program. What follows is a description of sacramental and traditional practices celebrated in the Mexican community and some mention of their significance. Lest the reader assume regional uniformity, the underlying fact of great variation in practices needs to be emphasized. This variety manifests itself especially when taking into account the region of Mexico or the United States of America where the persons originated, together with how much they have assimilated into the U.S. cultural mainstream and to the degree in which they participate in this mainstream culture. Particularly relevant here is the geographical distance that exists between the region where they now live and the Mexican border. Unlike the European migrations at the turn of the nineteenth century, many Mexican immigrants live much closer physically to their motherland, which allows greater physical mobility and psychological connectivity than the European immigrants possessed. While most European immigrants were clear that they were here to stay, the same may not hold true for the Mexican immigrant.

Some writers outline three areas through which the sacred manifests itself in the lives of Hispanics: (1) the sacramental constellation of practices (which corresponds to the official doctrine of the Church and serves to make the rites "seen and felt"); (2) the devotional constellation (which corresponds to the traditions of the Church relating to the saints); and (3) the constellation of protection (which corresponds to the Church's belief in miracles).[2] These three constellations, applied to Mexicans and Mexican-Americans, provide a framework for elaborating on the spirituality described above. These constellations occur within the Church's liturgical year, during which Mexicans participate in unique ways. Although these categories naturally overlap, thus demonstrating their connectedness, each accents a particular connection with the wider Church. For now, an overview of the liturgical year and the feasts of Mexican popular piety are in order.

The Liturgical Calendar and the Feasts of Popular Piety

Winter: Advent and Christmas Cycle

In the spirit of the Church's new liturgical year, Mexicans begin this holy season with Advent, a time of preparation for the Lord's coming at Christmas. Descendents of the indigenous and Iberian cultures, both of which have a special place for the role of motherhood, focus attention on the Blessed Mother as the central figure in the expectation of Christmas. Under the title of Our Lady of Guadalupe, whose feast is on December 12, she reflects the compassionate face of God.

At the time of her apparition in 1531, the indigenous peoples in Mesoamerica were overwhelmed by the Spanish conquest, which had brought both the cross and the sword to Mexico. War, famine, and diseases were devastating the indigenous population. Their traditions, customs, dances, and temples had been violently quashed. During this sad period in the history of the Americas an anonymous Aztec poet wrote, "We are crushed to the ground; we lie in ruins. There is nothing but grief and suffering in Mexico and Tlatelolco, where once we saw beauty and valor."[3] The image that the gentle Mother gave to Juan Diego, an indigenous convert to Christianity, was filled with intricate symbolism. The woman appeared in front of the sun and on top of the moon, both celestial objects worshipped by the ancient Aztecs, early inhabitants of the Mesoamerican valley. In this way she is depicted as being greater than both. The color of her cloak, together with its gleaming stars, marked her as a very important celestial being, as did the angel who carried her. Her face and hands were dark, like the people she had come to embrace. The black band around her waist revealed that she was pregnant, as the Spanish word *encinta* signifies. Therefore, the indigenous peoples knew that someone was yet to come.[4] Was she a goddess? Indeed not! Unlike other Aztec goddesses and gods, her gaze was downward, revealing her humility. Her hands reverently joined in prayer marked her as a creature praising her God, a God who was announcing that something new and wonderful was about to take place. She came, therefore, as an evangelizer, one who proclaimed the good news of Christ in both oral and visual languages that the native populations could understand.

Amid this great pain and suffering, the woman's face showed great compassion. Her words, spoken in Nahuatl, the Aztec language, demonstrated that she had come to reveal the loving, comforting presence of a God who was only being portrayed as powerful. "Let nothing frighten or distress you, do not let your heart be troubled...am I not here who am your Mother?"[5] Thus she comforted Juan Diego, the simple Indian convert to whom she appeared.

But her words, as is true of God's grace when manifested to an individual, were not meant for him alone. Juan Diego was sent on a difficult mission to the archbishop to arrange for him to build a place where others might come and be comforted in their sufferings and encouraged in their struggles. After a miraculous sign involving the image itself and Castilian roses, the archbishop complied. Today, more than 450 years later, that place, that sanctuary where the tired and discouraged can come to be renewed, remains a reality. But the reality is much bigger than a place. It is about a person who reflects the loving, comforting, maternal presence of a God who always grants us more than we can ask or imagine. During this period of the year, some people make the sacrifice of going on pilgrimage, or *peregrinación,* to this famous shrine in Mexico City. Local parishes throughout Mexico and the United States of America, desirous of serenading their Mother on her special day, bring her bouquets of roses and sing the *mañanitas* early in the morning before the break of dawn. The tradition of "flor y canto" continues. As one woman told her pastor who could not understand why it was necessary to spend so much for a live band of mariachis and get up so early: "Just think, Father, how happy our La Virgencita will be when we wake her up with our special morning serenade!"

Another popular custom is to enact the story of the apparitions, or Las Apariciones.[6] Some places also feature a procession and even a fiesta with folkloric dances. For many who, for whatever reason, have felt alienated from their land and their culture, this joyous celebration is a real homecoming. During the holy season of Advent, it is La Virgencita, the pregnant one, who helps us prepare for the coming of the Savior. Like John the Baptist, she is Advent personified because she prepares the way of the Lord. In the tradition of the prophets, she reminds us that the Juan Diegos of the world—the poor, the insignificant, the homeless, and the immigrant—are all Jesus waiting to be born.

Aside from the celebrations around Our Lady of Guadalupe, other Mexican practices around Advent and Christmas include Las Posadas, a nine-day novena that usually takes place in neighborhoods and enacts Joseph and Mary's search for lodging in Bethlehem; *La Pastorala* or *Los Pastores,* a mystery play of Spanish origin, filled with angels and devils, which centers on the shepherds' search to find the Child Jesus; La Misa de Gallo, or midnight Mass; La acostada del Niño, or the family practice of enthroning a statue of the Child Jesus in the home's *nacimiento,* or Nativity scene; El Día de los Reyes on January 6, the arrival of the magi, which was traditionally the day for gift giving; and finally, on February 2, La Candelaria, or Candlemas Day, the feast of the purification of Mary and of the presentation of the Child Jesus in the temple. On this day, candles—which are lit for protection on special occasions and under certain circumstances such as storms or a serious illness in the family—are blessed. With the exception of La Misa de Gallo, most of the celebrations take place in the home or the neighborhood. Many U.S. parishes, therefore, have found that helping to sponsor these is an excellent way to invite people in the neighborhoods to participate more fully in the life of the parish. There are also powerful reminders that spirituality is something practiced throughout our daily life and not just while we are in church.[7]

Such physical reminders as the decorations displayed during this holy season, whether they be *luminaries* (small, brown paper bags filled with sand and lit candles, prominently displayed along buildings and walkways on Christmas Eve, especially in New Mexico) or the *nacimiento* (the Christmas crib), help to communicate that the Word became flesh, entering into our time and our reality in order to dispel the darkness of sin and point us toward the way to life, a life lived in abundance. Special foods, such as *bunuelos* (fried pastries), tamales, or *empanaditas* (turnovers often filled with sweet spiced meat) add to festivities. For when a child receives candy after kissing the Baby Jesus, a practice I once saw in a church in San Antonio, we are reminded that "Dios está en todo" (God is in all things), and therefore, even despite difficulties, grace and sweetness abound.

Spring: Lent and Easter Time

Judging from the number of Mexicans and Mexican-Americans who come to receive ashes on Miercoles de Ceniza, or Ash Wednesday, one would conclude that this is the most important Church day of the year. In light of the fact that Palm Sunday also draws large crowds, so much so that a parish in Oakland, California, has had to schedule double the number of Masses for that Sunday, the humorous remark that "people love to come to church on those days because that's when they actually get something free" rings true! As *Faith Expressions* observes, "It [Ash Wednesday] is most important to the *mestizo* people who intuitively and symbolically recognize and affirm their close relationship to the earth, and the awareness of their own sinfulness and limitation."[8] Aside from the Church's call for prayer, penance, and almsgiving, Mexicans "live the season" through various practices which, like those around Christmas, often involve drama, such as El Vía Crucis, or the live Way of the Cross,[9] and special foods, such as *camarones* (shrimp), *nopalitos* (tender cooked cacti), and *capirotada* (a baked bread pudding of Spanish-Jewish origin). As *Faith Expressions* adds, "*kipper* and *Kapporet* are two Hebrew root words associated with the Jewish feast of the Atonement, Yom Kippur."[10]

Many Latino parishes sponsor *misiones,* or a series of Lenten talks aimed at spiritual renewal. These sessions will often be directed to specific groups such as children, youth, married couples, or sometimes to women and men separately.

This holy season climaxes with La Semana Santa, or Holy Week. In the Via Crucis and some other devotions of that week, El Nazareno, the suffering Jesus, and La Dolorosa figure prominently. In some places, for example, there is a service held in the evening of Good Friday, known as "el pésame a la Virgen," in which the community expresses its condolences to the Sorrowful Mother. Another popular practice that day is "el sermon de las siete palabras," or the sermon of the Seven Last Words, often lengthy reflections based on Jesus' words from the cross, which are often interspersed with hymns and prayers. "El servicio del santo entierro" is a type of solemn funeral procession with an image of the dead Christ.[11]

The day after, Holy Saturday, is sometimes called "el sábado de Gloria" because in the days before the Easter Vigil was put back on Saturday evening, it used to be held in the morning. At the singing of the Gloria at Mass, the veils that covered the main altar and the statues during Holy Week were removed and bells were rung triumphantly. It was not uncommon to have a dance that evening celebrating the end of Lent and the arrival of Easter. Another custom associated with this joyous time is that of the *encuentro,* or the early morning encounter between the risen Lord and his Mother, which is symbolized when the two statues of Jesus and Mary, each coming from a different direction, meet outside the church and are carried in procession to begin the joyful liturgy. In general, today the Easter Vigil is celebrated according to the official liturgy, with its vibrant symbolism of water, flowers, light, fire, and the assembly proclaiming vividly that a new era has dawned. Probably a new occurrence is the presence of adult Mexican-Americans who will be baptized or confirmed, given that it is becoming more common, especially among more assimilated persons, to delay baptism. Many families still practice the custom of having picnics on Easter Sunday.

The rest of the spring is taken up, in some communities, by having little girls offer flowers to Mary in May, and celebrating first communion on Mother's Day. In Mexico, Mother's Day is always celebrated on May 10. It is not uncommon to begin to serenade the mothers in their homes after midnight. It is interesting to note that Father's Day, while celebrated, does not command the same attention.

Summer and Fall: Feasts of the Saints

Part of the relationality in Mexican spirituality mentioned in the previous chapter, aside from a special bond with the Blessed Mother because of who she is in relation to Jesus, includes kinship with the saints. As an elderly woman commented when the statues were taken out of the main body of her old mission church and put in a side chapel, "Poor Jesus, he must feel so alone without his friends!" The saints are seen as powerful friends, advocates, and role models. Quite in sync with Catholic tradition, practically every profession and role in life has its own patron saint. St. Isidore, for example, is the patron of farmers. In a farming community, his feast will be important. What happens to that community, however, when it becomes more industrial? In a way, that shift is what is happening all over the United States of America, as the majority of Latinos/as no longer live in rural areas but in the cities.

Yet, at least among Catholic Mexicans, saints, whether canonized or not, continue to play an important role. Among the more popular ones are San Martín de Porres (1579–1639), a humble Dominican brother who lived a life of service to the very destitute in colonial Lima, Peru;[12] San Antonio de Padua (1195–1231), a Franciscan friar and doctor of the Church also known for his love for the poor; Santa Ana, according to tradition the mother of Mary; and Santa Monica (323–387), patron of mothers because she never stopped believing that her son, who became St. Augustine (354–430), would one day be converted. As elsewhere in different parts of the world, St. Jude Apostle (first century), the patron of hopeless causes, and St. Joseph, foster father of Jesus and patron of fathers, are also popular.

Saints, such as San Martín de Porres and Santa Rosa de Lima (1586–1617), the first canonized saint in and from the New World, who often appear in Latin American religious art, are very symbolic because they were born and lived in the Americas, just as St. Elizabeth Ann Seton (1774–1821) is in the United States of America. In a way, these saints further the sense that we, too, are holy, because these persons have lived among us and we can imitate what they did, especially in regards to taking care of the poor. An image of San Martín Caballero (St. Martin of Tours), a fourth-century pagan Roman soldier who became a Christian monk and bishop, is often seen hanging in small, commercial establishments. He is usually shown sharing his cloak with a poor, elderly beggar. Legend has it that the night he did that, he had a dream in which he saw Christ wearing the covering; thus, what he had done for the beggar, he had done for the Lord himself. His image serves as a reminder to treat the poor with dignity as did San Martín.

Among new immigrants, especially persons who are undocumented and are attempting to enter the United States of America illegally to provide for their families, two twentieth-century figures are becoming increasingly popular. One was officially canonized by Pope John Paul II in the year 2000—San Toribio Romo, a priest shot to death by soldiers in Jalisco, Mexico, during the Cristero War of the 1920s[13]—and one is simply honored by the people—Juan Soldado, who is buried in a cemetery in Tijuana. According to popular belief, Juan Castillo (Soldado) was a simple foot soldier who was falsely accused of violating and killing a young lady. He was subsequently executed. According to a journalist's report,

> During the entire day, pilgrims visit his tomb which has become a type of altar to him... Scrawlings reveal numerous miraculous events in the lives of poor persons: money for an operation, employment, help in order to get one's husband out of jail or one's son to stop drinking. When the petition has been granted, the faithful return in gratitude to offer flowers or to place a candle or a stone plaque announcing the favor.[14]

Thus, the saints serve not only as role models but also as intercessors. If God wills a miracle, the faithful are convinced that it will be granted. But if not, as the saying goes, "Cuando Dios no quiere, santo no puede" (When God does not will it, the saint is not able [to perform the miracle]).

The Mexican celebration of El Día de los Muertos on November 2 (also known as the Day of the Dead or All Souls' Day) is becoming increasingly well known throughout different regions of the United States of America as Mexicans bring this custom from their native land. On El Día de los Muertos they remember and commemorate family and friends who are deceased. Despite the sobriety of death, the spirit of the day is often a jovial one, punctuated by special candies and breads, some made in the shape of skulls and crossbones.[15] It is not uncommon to see families at the cemetery that day, decorating and cleaning the graves of their loved ones, spending time in prayer, and, at times, sharing a meal on the gravesite. Home altars, topped with pictures of the deceased surrounded by flowers, candles, and reminders of the persons, including at times, their favorite food or drink, are sometimes constructed in the home.

Alejandro García-Rivera sees this celebration as a family reunion.[16]

An emerging phenomenon is the celebration of El Día de los Muertos through museum and school exhibitions, as well as parades and other social events and fiestas. There may or may not be collaboration with a specific church. Reporting on the way it was celebrated in a specific community in Los Angeles, Lara Medina and Gilbert R. Cadena demonstrate how the festivities assembled a diverse crowd.

> Although there was little interaction between the "churched" and "unchurched" on the day of the communal ritual celebrations, the collaborative project between a parish community and secular cultural institutions proved beneficial in many ways. Religious and cultural workers joined in devoting their time to drawing out the wisdom and artistic skills of a struggling community. Adults and youth participated in the making of the ritual, activities that reinforce self-determination and community solidarity. In this context, cultural knowledge becomes sacred knowledge as people engage in the process of identifying what for them holds ultimate value. For Chicanas/os estranged from Catholicism, collaboration with church representatives provided a sense of relief that their traditions were finally being respected. Said one participant, "I remember being chastised for going to Mass and wearing a T-shirt that had a calavera [skull] face on it. The priest told me it was a demonic tradition...maybe they are finally listening to us.[17]

Indeed, listening and respectfully discerning the presence of God in the faithful is a monumental, but extremely necessary, pastoral skill.[18]

The Feast of Christ the King, celebrated at the end of the liturgical year, takes on special importance for many Mexicans. As mentioned in chapter 1, the Cristero Rebellion, a manifestation of the heated Church-state rivalry in the 1920s and 1930s, was a very difficult time for the Church in Mexico. Many martyrs, both lay and religious, such as the Jesuit priest Miguel Pro,[19] confidently stood before firing squads and uttered the famous cry, "Viva Cristo Rey!" (Long live Christ the King!). At a time when many peasants felt betrayed by their revolutionary leaders and the Catholic professional class, the only one who had not abandoned them was Christ the King.

A brief overview of the liturgical year with special attention to Mexican feasts and customs reveals that, surprisingly, many of the traditions from Mexico have endured. Parts of the reason for this continuity are the continued migrations coupled with the relative proximity of the country.[20] Yet, as Medina and Cadena's treatment of El Día de los Muertos reveals, these traditions are constantly evolving and therefore taking on new forms.[21] As a summary of the celebrations and customs that have been presented so far, as well as a conclusion to this chapter, what follows is a brief description of what some describe as the three constellations of popular piety.

The Three Constellations of Popular Piety

The Sacramental Constellation of Practices

The authors of *Faith Expressions of Hispanics in the Southwest* describe this category as embracing "those sacraments and sacrament-like or related rites which are close to the heart of Hispanics. There are three sacraments which enjoy great popularity among the Spanish-speaking peoples and which, in a way, mobilize the family. They are Baptism, First Holy Communion, and Matrimony."[22] Since the booklet's publication in 1977, other pastoralists have penned many articles and a book on these rites,[23] particularly through the efforts the Instituto de Liturgia Hispana, founded in 1979.[24] While an extensive treatment is not possible here, a mention of the unique elements in each of these three sacraments, as outlined by *Faith Expressions*, will hopefully convince the reader of their relevance. *Primero Dios* provides an in-depth explanation of each of these terms and how they function pastorally.[25]

> a. *Baptism* is a time when spiritual and familial ties are forged and reinforced around the celebration of a new birth. There is a special bond known as *compadrazgo,* for instance, between the parents of the child and the godparents. There is usually a fiesta that follows the ceremony, often enlivened by the custom of *bolo,* or the practice of throwing coins in the air for eager children to collect (a reminder of the graciousness and abundance of the baptismal waters), and/or that of the piñata.
>
> b. *First holy communion* celebrates when the child is invited to the Eucharistic table for the first time and marks another rite of passage. In some places there is the custom of also having *padrinos,* or godparents, present; these may or may not be the same as those at baptism. Some parishes have the children carry candles and renew their baptismal vows. Again, a fiesta at home usually follows, accompanied by more formal photographs later in the day.

c. *Matrimony,* celebrated as a sacrament within the church, may often be put off until the family has sufficient financial resources. It will usually involve more family participation than is often the case in other cultures within the United States of America. For example, although the couple ultimately decides to marry, many people still follow the custom that the parents of the groom ask the parents of the bride for her hand in marriage, a practice known as *pedir la mano.* The marriage rite itself incorporates *arras* (coins), which symbolize a desire to provide on the part of the groom and a willingness to practice good stewardship on the part of the bride. Given that many women are now also breadwinners, this symbolism is today sometimes altered to reflect the more mutual roles.[26] Another popular symbol is the *lasso,* a type of rosary that is put over the shoulders of the bride and the groom and "signifies their life commitment to each other and the bond which will unite their lives and love."[27] The witnesses are also called *padrinos,* and friends and family will also help sponsor the wedding festivities—for example, "la madrina del pastel" is the woman who provides the wedding cake. In terms of the legality of the marriage, the Mexican practice of requiring a civil ceremony before a religious one may seem odd to U.S. pastoral ministers in that the presiding priest or deacon fulfills the function for both church and state (although a civil license is required). Recent immigrants are often not aware of this practice in the United States of America.

d. *Other rites and sacraments* are usually connected with key moments in the lives of persons such as maturity, as in the case of the *quinceañera* or *quince años,* a type of "coming of age" for young women at fifteen years of age.[28] The celebration of these is quite controversial, even to the point where some pastors refuse to allow them to be celebrated. The Mexican American Cultural Center has put out an excellent bilingual ritual, complete with helpful pastoral notes, which addresses many of these questions.[29] As to the rites surrounding sickness and death, one of the most overriding ideals in the Latino culture is that, just as one needs the help of the community to be born into the world, so it is when one is physically leaving it.[30] While the festivities around El Día de los Muertos have already been described, it is important to keep in mind that they usually occur after a period of grieving. These activities at the time of death, known as *luto,* provide an opportunity for the family to grieve, a time when they are comforted by the prayers and emotional support of others, whether through visits, meals, or family prayer rituals such as rosaries *(el novenario)* or the anniversary Mass for the soul of the deceased. The authors of *Faith Expressions* make a cautionary note here: "An evangelization on the paschal dimension of death is in order for those who exaggerate or prolong the period of *luto.*"[31]

The Devotional Constellation of Prayers

Given what has been said already in regards to the faith traditions regarding Mary and the saints, and those concerning the different images of Christ, it is not necessary to go into further detail on this topic. Again, the element of relationality in Mexican spirituality weaves its way throughout these devotions.[32]

The Constellation of Protection and Petition Blessings

This aspect of Mexican or Hispanic spirituality most closely corresponds to the Church's belief in miracles.[33] Some pastoral theologians speculate that one of the reasons many Hispanics have left Roman Catholicism for Pentecostal or evangelical churches is that in a post–Vatican II more cerebral climate it is these newer churches that most stress belief in miracles. Similarly, these newer religious groups provide a clearer identity.[34] Pre–Vatican II spirituality, more medieval and less modern, stressed the emotive over the rational. To add to this reality, more traditional, less industrialized cultures often have a greater awareness of or appreciation for acknowledging the presence of suffering or evil in the world. When one's life is more predictable, a product of modern technology, such natural forces as weather, sickness, and death seem more distant. Not so for those who live in poorer, more vulnerable situations, where a drought or a flood can quickly destroy one's livelihood. To the extent that Mexican spirituality is still more "third world than first world," it calls upon the Almighty to provide basic sustenance and protection from all that is life-threatening.

This greater awareness of God's divine providence is the reason Mexicans, and to a lesser extent Mexican-Americans, seek blessings from the priest or their loved ones when traveling, in times of sickness, or at important occasions such as baptisms, weddings, or when approaching death. For example, it is customary for dying parents to bless their children. This blessing may extend to the articles associated with the event, such as when the priest or deacon is asked to bless the *recuerdos,* or mementos, which are given out by a family after a baptism, wedding, or anniversary of death celebration. Priests are often asked to bless persons, animals, objects, such as cars and religious objects, and places, particularly homes or places of business.[35]

As mentioned previously, sickness, impending surgery, pregnancy, a new job, migration, or a journey are special times when blessings are requested. The sense here is that it is precisely when we are most vulnerable that we have to seek God's abiding strength and protection. Coming from a period in which many children died at birth or soon after, some Mexican communities still take their newborns (or at times three-year-olds) to church for a blessing.[36] These blessings are requested in an individual, personal way. It is not uncommon, for example, for a person or a family to request a blessing after Mass despite the fact that the final blessing was just imparted to all present.

Oftentimes Mexicans coming from rural settings have a special love for animals, perhaps because of the indigenous sense of the sacredness of all of creation, not to mention the influence of the Franciscans! Where practiced, the blessing of animals reflects, according to the authors of *Faith Expressions,* "a deep desire for harmony with the animal kingdom and the whole world, and it anticipates the messianic times when the lion and the lamb will be lying together. It is a blessing of praise and thanks to God for protection and companionship of animals and their service to humankind."[37] It is another manifestation of "La vida es sagrada"!

Part of the constellation of protection includes the blessing of religious objects and places. It is not uncommon for a parish to have a small religious goods store where the faithful can purchase such objects as medals, rosaries, Bibles, crucifixes, statues, prayer books, and candles. Once again, these objects are often connected with such special occasions as baptisms, first communions, and weddings. Besides their use in the formal liturgy of the Church, and partly as an extension of it, water, candles, ashes, and palms are still very popular.[38]

Another element of this constellation is that of pilgrimages. This ancient practice, common to many of the world's great religions, provides an opportunity for the pilgrim to leave her or his environment and spend some quality time in a sacred site. In many ways, it provides both a retreat and a simple vacation for poor people. For Hispanics,

> it reflects their articulated affirmation of being a pilgrim people living out of the exodus to the promised land. The journey is often difficult because the place chosen for pilgrimage is usually remote. The sacrifice of time, effort, and energy—as well as of money—in order to arrive at the sacred place is part of the pilgrimage which is a special kind of prayer. The purpose of the pilgrimage is to *do* an act of prayer in adoration, thanksgiving, petition, and/or reparation. Sometimes the pilgrimage is a fulfillment of a promise, a *manda*.[39]

For Mexican Catholics on either side of the border, pilgrimages to such places as Nuestra Señora de San Juan de los Lagos (Our Lady of St. John of the Lakes) in Jalisco, Nuestro Señor de Chalma, about an hour-and-a-half by car from Cuernavaca, or to the most visited shrine in all of the Americas, the Basilica of Our Lady of Guadalupe in Mexico City, whether done as a parish, family, or individuals, can be very spiritually enriching. There are also pilgrimage sites in the United States of America, for example, the Santuarío de Chimayó in New Mexico and the shrine of La Virgen de San Juan de los Lagos in San Juan, Texas, which is especially popular among farm workers around the beginning and end of the migrant season. In places like San Juan de los Lagos in the state of Jalisco, Mexico, the local seminarians provide pastoral care for the pilgrims along the way (the journey may take days, weeks, or even months to complete). Often young people will walk or ride their bicycles for days to get there. On these occasions, people often go to confession, pray together as a family or parish group, and benefit from an experience of daily, intense Christian community life, not something to be taken for granted in times of growing secularization![40]

At times these pilgrimages are made to fulfill a promise known as a *manda* or a *promesa*.[41] The latter sometimes takes the form of a *juramento* (a solemn oath) and usually is done when the person is feeling overwhelmed by some addiction. It consists of making a solemn oath in the presence of one of the Church's ministers and then signing the back of a special holy card that specifies the period during which the person will abstain, usually from alcohol, but also from smoking or drugs. When friends try to get the person to imbibe these substances, she or he can resist by claiming to be *jurado* and by showing the holy card. This oath is not taken lightly: although there are some inherent dangers if the person does not have resources, such as Alcoholics Anonymous, to help cope with the addiction, and binge drinking may occur once the designated time is up, it has helped many people to immediately stop engaging in these self-destructive behaviors. Pastoral counseling with a person wishing to *jurar* should include a discussion of resources available and a plan for when the period, which is often three to six months, expires.

This brief overview of Mexican feasts and customs reveals an abundance of popular devotional practices, most of which are celebrated in sync with the Church's liturgical season and liturgy. The three so-called constellations of popular piety that are celebrated throughout the liturgical calendar incorporate sacraments, sacramentals, devotions to Christ, Mary, and the saints, blessings, prayers of petition, promises, and manifestations of gratitude into the Mexican's spiritual life. This popular religiosity is no longer simply a concern for pastoral theologians but is quickly becoming the very substance of an emerging Hispanic theology. While there can definitely be a "shadow side" to any popular piety, especially in those cases where it is not liberating, as when a family fears that they will be punished by God because they have not been able to fulfill their promise, or *manda*, far too often it has been dismissed as being overly emotional, superstitious, or too syncretistic to take seriously.[42] Stressing the need to take popular religion seriously, the author of one of the most widely used books on Hispanic ministry, Allan Figueroa Deck, nonetheless speaks of the tension often present around its incorporation in the U.S. Catholic Church.

> Sensitivity to Hispanics requires exposure to the people, knowledge about their history and way of being. It also means that one must appreciate the role of symbol, ritual, and narrative in their lives. The experience of a relatively rigid and highly univocal, standardized U.S. Catholicism must concede more than a little to the deeply expressive, graphic, polyvalent, and anomalous religiosity of the people. This has been no small leap for Catholics schooled in mainstream theology and pastoral studies in the decades after Vatican II. The clash continues in the area of esthetic taste, for example, in the liturgical norms that invoke simplicity and clarity when in fact the people prefer exuberance and variety.[43]

The fact remains that this popular religion is now one of the main themes being explored by Hispanic theologians.[44] This emerging theology is the subject of the following chapter.

Chapter 5

READING THE BIBLE IN SPANISH

AN EMERGING CONTEXTUAL THEOLOGY

Cuando Dios da, da a manos llenas.
(When God gives, God does so abundantly.)

One of my earliest memories of attending Catholic parochial school is that of a classmate in our almost exclusively Mexican-American environment. Brown bag lunches were eaten in the new, all-purpose building, which also served as our community's church. Across the school grounds lay the old mission church from the Spanish colonial era. On a particular day this classmate, whom I'll call Manuel, was eating his tasty burrito inside a paper bag so that no one would know what he had brought for lunch. It was a general consensus among the school children that a bologna sandwich on white bread (made with bleached enriched flour, no less!) was far superior to a homemade burrito, complete with salsa, one that a mother's loving hands had probably put together that very morning. The point of this anecdote is not that bologna sandwiches are devoid of taste, but that it is a shame that we school children, as evidenced by Manuel's embarrassment, could not freely enjoy, for whatever reason, one of our culture's most common foods: a delicious burrito made with beans, and sometimes meat (maybe after payday), eaten with flour tortillas made from scratch.

As I reflect upon this incident, which occurred over forty years ago, I rejoice that not only have our burritos come out of the paper bags, but also that they are being spread around for God's hungry people to be nourished. This concrete sharing of what Mexican-Americans bring to the Christian table is part of what is being called U.S. Hispanic or Latino/a theology. In a nutshell, it is an attempt to explore theology, which St. Anselm described as "faith in search of understanding," from a Hispanic perspective. This movement draws from both Latin America's theology of liberation, which has contributed much to our understanding of perspective in the way we do theology, as well as from theology done in the United States of America and Europe, for example, that surrounding feminism, ecumenism, and cultural studies.[1]

As theology currently being written in the United States of America, its sources are many. Like all good Christian theologies, it brings together the Scriptures, tradition (which includes Church teaching), and human experience. Latino/a theology goes beyond reflecting solely upon the Mexican religious experience (described in previous chapters) to include that of other Latin American groups. The fact that Mexican-Americans make up the largest group among them, however, to say nothing of the fact that Mexico is geographically closer, means that much of U.S. Hispanic theology draws heavily from the faith experience of Mexicans, although now in creative tension with other theologies and cultures. Although it is difficult to say exactly what this new theology is because it is still emerging, it is nonetheless possible to provide a general description of the shape it is taking and who some of its major writers are.

One of Several Contextual Theologies

Although their presence goes back to a time even before the founding of the United States of America, only recently have Hispanic voices started to be heard in theological circles. For over thirty years now scholars have been "doing theology" from a Hispanic perspective, a perspective frequently characterized by poverty and marginalization.[2] Latin America's theology of liberation has contributed much to our understanding of perspective in theological methodology. Protestant Hispanic theologian Justo González, trying to propose a more contextualized biblical theology, calls this approach "reading the Bible in Spanish." By this expression González does not mean literally reading the Bible in a Spanish translation but bringing to the interpretation of Scripture a particular perspective. He hopes that such a perspective will help not only Hispanics but also the Church at large.[3]

To the extent that Latino/a theology proceeds from an acknowledgment and affirmation of its particular context in history, it is considered one of the many "contextual theologies" presently being developed. Justo González describes the emergence and common characteristics of these theological currents that are presently enjoying a great deal of popularity among Christians throughout the world.

> In the second half of the twentieth century, as the pool of those pursuing theological studies and reflection became increasingly diverse, it became apparent that every theologian's social and economic context leaves its mark on that person's theology. Thus arose a series of theologies that, rather than denying their contextuality, affirmed it, claiming that this provides new and valuable insights into the meaning of Scripture, of the gospel, and of doctrines in general. These various forms of theology are often called

"contextual theologies," even though they claim that every theology is of necessity contextual, and that a theology that claims to be universal and free of every contextual bias is simply blind to its own contextuality.[4]

According to contextual theologians, the strength of focusing on a particular context, as well as the realization that one cannot do good theology otherwise, is that one is able to "draw parallels between their own situation and that of biblical writers, and thus claim to gain a particular valuable insight into the meaning of the text."[5] An immediate example that comes to mind is how the African-American slaves had a better insight into the exodus of the children of Israel than their masters. Some liberation theologians have referred to this insight or ability to understand at a deeper level as the "hermeneutical privilege of the poor" (hermeneutics having to do with the tools used to interpret a text).

Justo González, acknowledging that there can be as many contextual theologies as there are human contexts, nonetheless lists several that are making their presence felt in theological circles, thus engendering a conversation, not only with each other but with more traditional forms. Among them, he cites black theology, Latin American theology, feminist theology, womanist theology (done by African-American women), *mujerista* theology (one of the forms of Latina theology), *minjung* theology (a type of Korean liberation theology), and Latino/Hispanic theology.[6] These forms of doing theology, which reflect a renewed dialogue with cultures and the human condition, could not have come about without a major shift in our theological method.

Origins

Some of the first Hispanic theologians were not as much concerned about making a contribution to the wider Church as they were about developing a theology and pastoral practice to help guide ministry to Hispanics. Many consider Virgil Elizondo to be the major pioneer of Hispanic theology. He first gained wide acclaim for his reflections on religion and culture.[7] The Mexican-American priest from San Antonio, Texas, describes what it was like to grow up living between two very different worlds: the Mexican and the American. While early memories of basking in the warmth of a Mexican-American community evoke a paradise, later years brought feelings of rejection and discrimination from Anglo culture.

> The paradise existence of the neighborhood came to a halt the first day I went to a Catholic grade school operated by German nuns in what had been a German parish. There the pastor still told Mexicans to go away because it wasn't their church. My parents had sent me there because it was the nearest Catholic school. Mexicans were tolerated but not very welcome.[8]

In another passage from his autobiographical work, Elizondo reflects on how he came to see himself, not in terms of someone who didn't belong, whether as a "pure Mexican" or a "pure American," but in terms of something entirely new.

> Between the school years at the seminary and the summers at the store [the family business located in a Mexican neighborhood], I gradually became more and more aware of the many things that I was not; I was not and would never be, even if I

wanted to, a regular U.S.-American. Yet neither would I be a *puro mexicano*. There were identities that I knew that I was and was not at the same time: U.S.-American, Mexican, Spanish, Indian. Yet I was! My very being was a combination. I was a rich mixture but was not mixed-up! In fact, I was more and more clear that my own inner identity was new and exciting. I started to enjoy the feeling of who I was: I was *not just* U.S.-American and *not just* Mexican but fully both and exclusively neither. I knew both perfectly even though I remained a mystery to them. And I was threatening to them since they knew I knew them, but they did not know me fully. I lived in two worlds, and the two worlds lived in me. That was wealth.[9]

From this personal insight, Elizondo moved to grappling with the larger picture. In the final chapter, "Towards Universal Mestizaje," he describes a mixture, or *mestizaje,* not only at the cultural level but also at the religious one.[10] Jesus is described as the great universalizer.

The radical universalizing newness of the way of Jesus of Nazareth is that it offers people the possibility of a hyphenated existence: Jewish-Christians, Gentile-Christians, Afro-Christians, Asian-Christians, *Mestizo*-Christians. Thus the way of Jesus affirms local identity while opening it up to fellowship and free exchange with all others. Jesus' way is the opposite of the abstract universals of philosophy or ideology; it is concrete, specific sociocultural identity no longer threatened by others or afraid of being contaminated by others.[11]

This *mestizaje* is not one of dominance but rather one of cultural and religious pluralism, a combination of the particular and the universal. Through the integration of various cultural riches, people become more human and therefore more Christian. This notion of *mestizaje,* which speaks of the in-between-ness of this part of the population, similar to Jesus' own status as a Galilean, a group that was looked down upon in his time, has become paradigmatic for Latino/a theology.

What follows are other important aspects of the faith experience of Mexican-Americans, especially as being articulated by Hispanic theologians, some of whom are of Mexican descent and others who reflect on the experience of this group that makes up the largest sector of the U.S. Latino population. Following Elizondo's example, a handful of others have begun to create a theology rooted in the Latino experience of Church.[12] The year 1974 saw the publication of two articles, one by the Jesuit priest Allan Figueroa Deck and the other by Marina Herrera, an expert on multicultural catechesis.[13] Deck and Arturo Bañuelas, a diocesan priest from El Paso, Texas, helped bring together these academicians to form the Academy of Hispanic Theologians (ACHTUS) in 1988.[14] Just as Latin America's theology of liberation opened new horizons in terms of its systematic contributions in Christology and ecclesiology, for example, U.S. Hispanic theologians hope to do the same by starting to write about such subjects as grace, sin, the Trinity, sacraments, Christian anthropology, Mariology, and ecclesiology—always within the context of persons who form part of a community with a living tradition. The great theological categories, therefore, are messages addressed to the life of the community, not simply the individual in isolation, which has become the curse of much of modern culture.

Method

Much of current theology's shift to the human person, described in some ways as a concern for the particular as opposed to the disengaged universal, has meant less of an emphasis on orthodoxy ("right thinking" or doctrine) and more on orthopraxis ("right acting"). The theologians who are concerned that too much has been said about orthodoxy and not enough about orthopraxis are convinced that "praxis is just as important as proper doctrine—or rather, that a doctrine, no matter how correct, that does not lead to and derive from the praxis of love is flawed."[15]

In general, Hispanic theologians use the praxis approach advocated by liberation theology. At the same time, they are also cognizant of the danger of trying to import uncritically what is best suited for another context. They are theologizing, therefore, from a unique cultural perspective, more concretely, from the position within which they, as members of an oppressed people, experience God.[16] This new group of theologians, of which a significant number are women, seems intuitively aware of the need to stay in touch with the theological environment that gave them birth. At the same time, however, they are responding to the challenge to dialogue with the tradition as presented by more mainstream or so-called academic theologians.

Such works often start from looking at the socioeconomic reality, and proceed to use the "see, judge, act method," that is, the circle of moving from the experience of insertion into the situation's reality, doing social analysis and examining that reality through the eyes of faith, finally, moving toward pastoral planning.[17] Two key works that engage a praxis methodology are *Hispanic Women: Prophetic Voice in the Church* by Ada María Isasi-Díaz, a Cuban-American, and Yolanda Tarango, a Mexican-American; and *The*

Second Wave: Hispanic Ministry and the Evangelization of Cultures by Allan Figueroa Deck.

In the fall of 1986, Isasi-Díaz published "'*Apuntes*' for an Hispanic Women's Theology of Liberation," an article that set the tone for the evolution of *mujerista* theology.[18] Soon after, together with Yolanda Tarango, a Sister of Charity of the Incarnate Word from El Paso, Texas, she produced a work that is destined to be a classic for its methodological innovation. In *Hispanic Women: Prophetic Voice in the Church,* the two Latina theologians expound their theory of what constitutes a theology from the perspective of Hispanic women and proceed to illustrate this process with examples. Their approach was to reflect with groups of Hispanic women to learn and understand their beliefs about the Divine.[19]

From what emerged during these discussions, they sought to identify recurring themes. Since they maintain that *mujerista* theology is a liberative praxis, behavior remains an important constituent. The researchers, therefore, consequently examined the ethical understandings of these Hispanic women, also looking to derive recurrent themes. The final part of the process included feedback to the contributors for the purpose of verifying that, in fact, what the researchers recorded and analyzed was representative of their beliefs and for it to be integrated into future liberative praxis. Yolanda Tarango and Ada María Isasi-Díaz have adopted this method, which in many ways is quite anthropological, for doing theology. This "let the women speak for themselves" approach guards against an idealized community perspective when speaking about Hispanics. At the heart of dealing with one's own historical subjectivity are self-awareness and consciousness. This self-reflective process is key to doing *mujerista* theology. It is a way of taking seriously the faith experience, or as Isasi-Díaz labels it, the "lived experience" of Hispanic women. From the beginning,

Isasi-Díaz and Tarango make it clear that their goal is liberation. Thus they make no pretensions of proceeding from an objective, passionless stance.

> First and foremost we are activists—Hispanic Women committed to the struggle for justice and peace. Our lived experience has pointed us in the direction of being theologians. We see no conflict in being both theologians and activists; this follows our understanding of the intrinsic unity between what has been classically referred to as systematic theology and moral theology or ethics. This will become obvious as we clarify what it means for us to *do* theology.[20]

Isasi-Díaz's later book, *En la Lucha/In the Struggle: Elaborating a Mujerista Theology,* uses the same methodology to further elaborate a *mujerista* theology. The overall impression one gets from reading it, along with *Hispanic Women: Prophetic Voice in the Church,* is the need to take seriously the emotive when theologizing.[21] Isasi-Díaz and Tarango take to heart anthropologist Clifford Geertz's definition of religion as

> a system of symbols which acts to establish powerful, pervasive, and long-lasting moods and motivations in men by formulating conceptions of a general order of existence and clothing these conceptions with such an aura of actuality that the moods and motivations seem uniquely realistic.[22]

The stories told by the women Isasi-Díaz and Tarango interviewed, whose recurring themes often involve community and family, reveal much of the "moods and motivations" behind their belief, as well as their ethical behavior.[23]

Like Isasi-Díaz and Tarango, Mexican-American Allan Figueroa Deck is extremely concerned about praxis. Theory is at the service of practice and practice must influence theory.[24] The Jesuit's most commented-on work to date is *The Second Wave: Hispanic Ministry and the Evangelization of Cultures.*[25] Through this work, Deck has constructed a framework for understanding Hispanic ministry in the Catholic Church today. It is an effort to surface pastoral issues. By "Second Wave" Deck is referring to the demographic trend of Latin Americans and Asian-Pacific peoples to the United States that started after World War II and continues to today. This progressive trend has been changing the face of the U.S. Catholic Church. Once heavily populated by immigrants or their descendents chiefly from Europe, tomorrow's U.S. Catholic Church will be Hispanic or Latino in the majority.

Deck notes that the "first wave" of immigrants to the United States of America consisted of the traditionally Catholic ethnic groups—Irish, German, Italian, and Slavic. In many ways, these groups assimilated well into the U.S. cultural mainstream.

> U.S. Catholics have become comfortable with their hard-earned identity. Sons and daughters of the teeming masses—the "first wave"—that disembarked in the last century or early in this one, they achieved acceptance in a predominantly Protestant and rather anti-Catholic country. The struggle was long and often bitter. World War II gave these immigrants and their offspring an opportunity to demonstrate their Americanism. They performed their civic and patriotic duties

with distinction. By and large, they ceased speaking their native languages. And by 1960 the United States was able to elect a Catholic president. Roman Catholics were becoming "as American as apple pie."[26]

But with the more recent arrival of the large new groups of immigrants, many of whom are Catholic, the Church has found itself in a different position.

At this moment in time, consequently, the U.S. Catholic Church is schizophrenic, caught between two identities. One is the achievement of the mainstreaming process; the other is the result of a new migration that shows no sign of abating. This migration will transform that Church by the next century into a predominantly Hispanic American institution just as today it is predominantly Irish American.[27]

From the beginning, Deck sets the stage for what today is the most important challenge for the Church in the United States of America: "This book is written with the conviction that what is done to promote the effective pastoral care of Hispanics today will determine to a degree still not fully appreciated the vitality and effectiveness of the U.S. Catholic Church of the twenty-first century."[28] Sheer numbers, to say nothing of the challenge of the gospel, dictate a careful revision of pastoral strategy that takes into account not only the good of the Hispanic community but also that of the entire U.S. Church. For Deck, a true evangelization of the North American Church calls for a consistent attentiveness to such gospel values as mutual respect, dialogue, and pluralism.[29]

In general, his writings reveal a mediation between theory and practice. That is, he brings theological sources, such as the Bible, present reality, and the magisterium, to bear on practical issues and practical concerns to bear on theological sources. For example, in writing about illegal migration into the United States of America, he engages theological and biblical concepts regarding aliens, Catholic social teaching, and present sociological reality.[30]

While this section has described the two Mexican-Americans' (as well as a Cuban-American's) approach to theology through the lens of praxis, there are Hispanic writers whose method is more in dialogue with anthropology, philosophy, and art. Their method emerges out of their grappling with several major themes that are summarized below. Some, such as Our Lady of Guadalupe and the religious meaning behind the concept of fiesta, have already been discussed.

Major Theological Themes Found in Latina/o Writings on Mexican Topics

Popular Religion or Religiosity

The Latino theologian who has written the most on this important thread of Hispanic theology is Orlando O. Espín. Born in Cuba and reared in the United States of America, he has worked in the Dominican Republic and Brazil, as well as in the United States of America. He is also founding editor of the *Journal of Hispanic/Latino Theology*. Because his theological reflections emerge partly from the Mexican religious reality, especially as it relates to popular piety, his work is summarized here. Espín, whose main medium of expression has been through articles and conferences, has distinguished himself through his reflections on the role of culture in theology and the importance of incorporating popular religiosity in theological work.[31] He has dealt with such topics in systematic theology as grace, sin, the Trinity, and Christian anthropology. He argues that popular religiosity, which he considers to be a privileged means of understanding the *sensus fidelium*, is a key source for constructing an adequate theology of grace and providence. By *sensus fidelium*, Espín refers to the living witness of the faith of the people, that is, a certain intuition that springs from a Christian way of life.[32] In light of the long history of Mexican-American and Latin American spirituality, the theologian's assertion that "popular religiosity is a privileged vehicle for Hispanic cultures" makes sense.[33] This "least invaded cultural creation" provides a means for preserving the faith. In his words: "It is through popular religiosity that we have been able to develop, preserve, and communicate deeply held religious beliefs. Through it we experience profound encounters with God."[34]

Like Deck, Espín bemoans the lack of serious attention given to the study of popular religiosity on the part of modern theologians. Often perceived as pertaining to the work of anthropologists or social scientists, the role of popular religiosity in the Church has been downplayed even by some liberation theologies. Espín notes, "It is no exaggeration to say that, in Catholic theological circles, popular religion is either treated as an example of what should not be, or it is simply ignored as of no value for the serious theological enterprise."[35]

In an interview with the *National Catholic Reporter*, Espín explicates the difference in an approach where popular Catholicism is studied "not as an anthropologist would study it, but as a theologian."[36] He continues, describing some of the characteristics of this popular religiosity, including "an emphasis on compassion and solidarity, an emphasis on the affective and, literally on the popularity of it—it's people's Catholicism," with clergy less important than laity as leaders.[37]

In his writings, Espín singles out two key symbols found in popular religiosity, symbols he calls "bearers of the Christian gospel": the crucified Christ and Mary. "These two symbols are present in every Catholic Hispanic community in the United States with very similar functions and meaning, giving us a religious connecting link amid Hispanic diversity."[38] Over the centuries, the suffering Christ, as evidenced by Hispanic iconography and popular devotions such as those focused on the passion, has appealed to Latinos. Espín explains why, linking the history of oppression with an intuitive sense of the transformative power of the cross today.

> The Christ of Hispanic passion symbolism is a tortured, suffering human being. The image leaves no room for doubt. This dying Jesus, however, is so special because he is not just another human who suffers unfairly at the hands of evil humans. He is the divine Christ, and that makes his innocent suffering all the more dramatic. He is prayed to as one speaks with a living person, and not merely mourned or remembered as some dead hero of the past. His passion and death express his solidarity with all men and women throughout history who have also innocently suffered at the hands of evildoers.[39]

Elsewhere, the Cuban-born theologian, after having examined historically some of the means used in the early evangelization of indigenous Mexico, illustrates why the crucified Christ became so popular: a vanquished people could relate to a suffering Christ. Incorporating history, anthropology, and theology, Espín masterfully relates this suffering Christ to Trinitarian monotheism in sixteenth-century Mexico.[40]

Role of Women

María Pilar Aquino, born in Ixtlán del Río, Nayarit, grew up in Sonora, Mexico, and was educated in Mexico, Costa Rica, Peru, and Spain. She bears the distinction of being the first Catholic woman to obtain a doctorate in theology from the Pontifical University of Salamanca, Spain. Her publications are extensive. Her first book, *Aportes para una Teología desde la Mujer,* was an edited work.[41] In 1992 she published *Nuestro Clamor por la Vida: Teología Latinoamericana desde la Perspectiva de la Mujer.*[42] A fuller version of this work, *Our Cry for Life: Feminist Theology from Latin America,* was published in 1993 in English.[43]

Aquino is attempting to develop a theology of liberation from the viewpoint of Latinas.[44] Her article, "Doing Theology from the Perspective of Latin American Women,"[45] summarizes ideas that are expanded in her book. At the core of her work is a critique of some of the dominant theological methods employed today, including that of some Latin American liberation and U.S. Hispanic theologians. Like Isasi-Díaz, whose *mujerista* theology prompts her to make a distinction between North American and Latina feminism, Aquino is critical of the North American. In presenting her essay, the editor, Roberto S. Goizueta, makes the following remarks:

> Sympathetic to Latin American liberation theology and Anglo American feminism, Aquino nevertheless proffers a critique of both: the first for its male-centered perspective, and the latter for its failure to make explicit the causal link between sexism and classism, between the privileges of First World women and the exploitation of Third World women. Such a critique is essential as Latinas

develop a theological reflection which affirms them as historical subjects in their own right. In turn, this reflection contributes to the development of an integral theological perspective which will be liberating for both women and men.[46]

Aquino also shares with Isasi-Díaz a criticism of a theology that does not take the affect seriously along with one that is not based on lived experience.[47]

Two realities become increasingly obvious as one reads her writings: (1) within one of the poorest minority groups in the United States of America (although her frame of reference includes all of Latin America), Latinas are among the most needy and oppressed;[48] and (2) Latinas are, in reality, the driving force behind most of the work being done in evangelization and social advocacy today. To substantiate the first reality, that of the oppression of Latina women, she quotes I. Gebara, who asserts that in Latin America

the poor have many faces: laborers, farmworkers, beggars, abandoned children, the marginalized and dispossessed youth, and others. They are men and women, but among them we should give precedence to one group: *the women*…The poor woman today is poor even among the poor. She is truly other: the overburdened woman, the menstruating woman, the laboring woman, mother, daughter, and wife. She is at the same time, both subject and object of our option for the poor.[49]

When one considers the number of Latin American women who, in order to provide for their families, are forced to migrate to developed countries, especially to the United

States of America, her description quickly becomes applicable to a North American context.

To this reality, Aquino brings the light of the gospel, a gospel that proclaims life in all its fullness. It is this promotion of the gospel and of life that should be the locus of theology.

> The aim of theology from the point of view of women must share the aim of God's re-creative activity in history and must be inspired by it. Moreover, it must illuminate and activate the response of faith by the one who embraces it. In accordance with the core of the liberating biblical vision, this aim is on the path toward the attainment of the fullness of life, human integrity, shared solidarity, complete liberation, and common enjoyment of the goods of the earth. The biblical formulation of this aim is found succinctly in John 10:10: "I have come that they may have life, and that they may have it abundantly."[50]

Despite their poverty and oppression, Aquino demonstrates how these faith-filled Latinas are not without hope. Far from it, they are heavily involved in the transformation of both the society and of the Church.

> For Latina women, Christian faith is not a fragmentary aspect of their life or of their own cultural identity. The struggle of these women for a new earth and for new ways of being and living in the church, where they can participate as members in their own right, is inspired by their conviction of faith, and affects their whole life. To state just a few of their activities, many Latina women are committed to human rights groups, to the defense

of the undocumented, to solidarity movements, to peace, to ecological, artistic, and cultural movements, to liberating evangelization groups, to the affirmation of indigenous communities, to the defense of civil rights, to the affirmation of women, young people, children, and the aged, and so on. Consequently, theological reflection must take into account their multiple interests as believers, as poor, and as women, together with their religious and cultural values.[51]

Given their oppressive situation, yet also their committed work for faith and justice, Aquino argues that Latinas have much to contribute to the theological enterprise. Yet, writing in 1992, she bemoans the lack of Hispanic women theologians, commenting that "it is absurd that after five hundred years of Christianity on this continent, there are less than eight Latin American women holding the doctoral degree in theology."[52] She is likewise critical of the lack of leadership opportunities available for women in Church settings.[53]

Aquino feels that some U.S. Hispanic male theologians, by their excessive concern for identity issues, along with those related to popular religiosity, are losing sight of the socioeconomic realities that characterize the Latino population, both in the United States of America and in Latin America. Her critique is that they are paying too much attention to cultural liberation and not enough to a socioeconomic one, thereby running the risk of not being in touch with the fullness of reality.

Beauty or Theological Aesthetics

Similar to Espín's concern that popular religiosity be seen as a *locus theologicus,* or the place where theology finds its sources, such as Scripture, tradition, or experience, Roberto

Goizueta, also Cuban-American, writes about the theological significance of such Mexican cultural realities as Our Lady of Guadalupe or perceptions of the suffering Christ.[54] His most famous work to date is *Caminemos con Jesús: Toward a Hispanic/Latino Theology of Accompaniment.*[55] In this and other writings, Goizueta is grappling with some of what is behind such a radical difference in perception and comportment for the Hispanic in comparison with other North Americans. While the history of oppression cannot be overlooked, something Elizondo has repeatedly pointed out, Goizueta focuses on philosophical propositions. He notes, for example, that the aesthetic paradigm has played an important role in the history of Latin American philosophy, in many ways, as an alternative to the Cartesian epistemological paradigm.[56] Popular religiosity, therefore, which engages the senses and not simply appeals to reason, will be more attractive than other ways of encountering the sacred.

This preference for the aesthetic paradigm does not deny the ability to be rational. Goizueta is critical of a certain tendency of U.S. dominant culture to stereotype Latinos.

> Portrayed as amiable, fun-loving people of warmth, feeling, and fiestas, i.e., people of "the body" over against the Anglo-Saxons, people of "the mind," we have been denied our minds and deemed incapable of serious, rational thought. Despite the fact that some of the greatest literature, philosophy, theology, poetry, etc. has been written in Spanish, the language itself continues to be perceived as less "scholarly" than French or German.[57]

While looking back at the great cultural heritage found in Spain and Latin America, Goizueta acknowledges the birth of a new people, the *mestizo* Elizondo has described so eloquently. It is within this new world and new context that the Latino theologian must work. Anthropology plays a crucial role in this process of contextualization.[58] Goizueta writes:

> By examining the nature of subjectivity and community from within a U.S. Hispanic worldview, and the consequent role of such an anthropology in U.S. Hispanic theological method, we will explore the significance of a Hispanic anthropology, or understanding of the person, for the theological method.[59]

The Cuban-born theologian is clear that a Hispanic contextual theology will not only reap benefits for Hispanics but also for the Church at large. One gets the sense that Goizueta, conscious of his own bicultural background, is exploring how the recent writings of U.S. Hispanic theologians fit into an intuitive schema that somehow sees theory, praxis, and the aesthetic as all being interrelated. According to Arturo Bañuelas, this combination of theory-praxis-aesthetic can be summarized as the cycle of knowing the truth (theory), doing justice (praxis), and feeling the beautiful (aesthetic).[60]

A New Ecumenism

This generation of Hispanic scholars has worked hard at bridging the wide gap between the Roman Catholic and Protestant Hispanic churches. Judging from their writings, one notes that they are familiar with each other's work. There has been a nuanced understanding of tradition as Hispanic Catholics have begun to recognize that they are not the only bearers of a particular type of cultural Christianity and Protestant Hispanics are becoming more aware of the Catholic tradition from which they still partake.[61]

Other signs of hope for an increased ecumenical understanding between the churches are becoming more evident.
Among the most notable are collaborative educational ven-
tures among the numerous ecumenical theological centers
throughout the country, for example, the Graduate Theological Union in Berkeley, California; the Hispanic Summer
Program, an annual two-week master's-level course of theological study, whose location rotates to different campuses
and is taught by Latino/a faculty; open collaboration in
terms of scholarly journals; and, finally, joint efforts for justice, especially in the case of inner-city, faith-based community organizing projects.[62]

The Relevance of U.S. Hispanic Theology
to a Larger Church Audience

As a subset of U.S. Hispanic or Latino/a theology, the
Mexican theological themes highlighted in this chapter—
popular religion or religiosity; the role of women, especially
in regards to justice; beauty or theological aesthetics; and
ecumenism—have much to contribute to our wider Church
context. In asking why this theology, so peculiar to a specific
context, should be of interest to a wider audience, Kenneth
Davis responds with five reasons: (1) history: "Catholicism
in what is now the United States did not begin with the original thirteen colonies but with the Spanish *Conquistadores*
and missionaries, indigenous nomads and architects, as well
as African slaves and shamans"; (2) demographics: "some
20 million Catholic Hispanics live in the United
States...hence, the percentage of Catholics in the United
States who are Hispanic is huge and exploding"; (3) cele-
bratory: "the distinctive way whereby Hispanics are
Catholics [as a product of Iberian, indigenous, African, and
U.S. cultures] has created a diverse and distinct way of being

Catholic"; (4) "common sense if not common decency": in a climate where politicians and businesses are desperate to get their attention, "perhaps Catholic strategic self-interest will be sufficient motivation to listen to Hispanic sisters and brothers if history, demography, spirituality, and justice are not"; and (5) the discipline of theology: a theological method that is communitarian, collaborative, connected with people's lived experience, and transformative. In terms of the formal discipline of theology, Davis concludes: "These are new paradigms for theology that challenge the liberal versus conservative stalemate as it creates a systematic synergy between theology and ministry that is an imaginative, meaningful contribution to the academy as well as the whole Church."[63]

Chapter 6

PASTORAL CHALLENGES AND OPPORTUNITIES

FREQUENTLY ASKED QUESTIONS REGARDING MINISTRY WITH AND AMONG MEXICANS AND MEXICAN-AMERICANS

Dios da, pero no acarrea.
(God gives but he does not carry, or God helps those who help themselves.)

It is not uncommon today to see in most computer programs or on Internet sites a section entitled "FAQs," or "frequently asked questions." This chapter attempts to be more user-friendly by offering concrete suggestions to pastoral realities using the same format. Like the Mexican proverb quoted above, this chapter provides practical wisdom for the pastoral agent. Chapter 2 pointed out the U.S. Mexican population's poverty, lack of formal education, and other socioeconomic factors. In subsequent chapters, reference was made to the U.S. Mexican community's youthful quality, strong family formation, spirituality, and emerging theology, which are signs of hope for this population within the U.S. Catholic Church. This chapter looks at a few of the pastoral challenges this community offers to the Church along with the many opportunities it presents. Much of the material comes from personal interviews with laypeople, religious, seminarians, and priests—many mentioned in the preface—who serve as pastoral agents and educators.

Before presenting these pastoral challenges and opportunities, fairness to our history as the U.S. Catholic Church necessitates our acknowledging that we stand on the shoulders of giants. As chapters 1 and 2 acknowledge, from the time of the first evangelization of the Americas beginning in the sixteenth century, gifted men and women have creatively dedicated themselves to the task of spreading the good news in the New World.[1] They strove to discern the "signs of the times" and to develop an inculturated catechesis and liturgy, one that would teach and embody gospel values in ways that native peoples could understand and embrace. Another historic event was the establishment of a national office for Hispanic ministry in 1945. The fact that today more than "75 percent of the dioceses have an office for Hispanic ministry, and almost four thousand parishes provide pastoral services to Hispanics in the Spanish language"[2] can be traced directly back to that one event. The preparation of so many persons to work in Hispanic ministry owes much to the pioneering work of such institutions as the Mexican American Cultural Center (MACC) in San Antonio, Texas.

The U.S. bishops, writing in *Encuentro & Mission: A Renewed Pastoral Framework for Hispanic Ministry*,[3] exhort Hispanics to assume leadership roles in a culturally diverse Church. Yet the fact remains that only 4 percent of trained lay ecclesial ministers are Hispanic, while only 5 percent of the priests in the United States of America are Hispanic.[4] Given these statistics, it is crucial that we revisit our histories, especially in light of the principles that guided these pastoral strategies.[5]

In designing a local pastoral plan for an immigrant Mexican population, what kinds of things should we keep in mind?

1. Get to know your congregation. A key factor is to find out as much as possible about the population that now lives in your community, especially in areas that previously had a small Hispanic presence, such as in New Orleans, Louisiana, following Hurricane Katrina in 2005. Find out about the native land—nationality, state, and village, if possible. Why is this important? In the case of persons who come from the very indigenous Mexican state of Oaxaca, for example, you might learn that Spanish is a second language for them. But you will also learn that each state and each community will often have its own customs and practices, just as people who come from different parts of the United States of America will have. How old are they?[6] While the majority of those coming in the past were young men determined to help out their families back in Mexico, it is now not uncommon to see women and even children at times. There are towns in Mexico in such states as Michoacán, for example, where the shortage of young men makes it very difficult for young women to find a husband. How long have they been in the United States of America, and how long do they plan to stay? Many Mexican immigrants to the United States of America are really migrants who come seasonally to work in agriculture or related businesses. Others come for much longer periods. While few Mexicans want to leave their country for a strange land in search of work to support their families, the availability of a job—even those considered demeaning by some U.S. residents—as well as the strength of the dollar against the Mexican peso, keeps them coming across the border despite the increasing danger and hardship.[7] The effects of poverty coupled with illegal immigration are marked: family disintegration, illiteracy, marital infidelity, crowding, exploitation, low self-esteem, and alco-holism, which is often connected to domestic violence. Also, most Mexican immigrants are expected to send money home to their families in Mexico, aside from providing for their own border crossing and living expenses in the United States of America.

One of the most difficult aspects of working with Mexican immigrants is that the minister quickly finds herself or himself being called upon to function in a religious role and as social worker, educator, therapist, nurse, lawyer, polit-ical advocate, and activist. This population, most often beset by poverty, lack of education, and legal residency complica-tions does not have the supports of other social classes in the United States of America. Social networks that tap into the communities' resources in these areas are invaluable. The pastoral minister, therefore, must develop a good list of pro-fessionals who can help—don't try to do it all by yourself! At times the realities of working with and among a Hispanic population that has more than its share of problems—AIDS, for example, is the fourth leading cause of death among Hispanic men and women aged twenty-five to thirty-four—can be overwhelming.[8]

2. **Encourage them as much as possible.** Given the many difficult factors described above, it is no wonder that these recently arrived communities do not immediately take to parish life as lived in the United States of America. Their experience of religion and spirituality, often connected with domestic practices of popular religiosity, given the demands of work and school, is dramatically altered. That is why such practices as the *posadas* and the celebrations around Our Lady of Guadalupe, described in chapter 4, can take on a new meaning for them. These become a way of reconnecting with their native communities, as well as passing on their liv-ing traditions to their children amid what they perceive as

secularizing trends. When these celebrations are not given as much importance as they were back home, or when they are not celebrated as "big" as they might be in their Mexican pueblos, people can become discouraged. That is where pastoral leadership is key in helping them to realize that it takes time to create the kind of religious community they experienced back home. Their progress in doing the same in the United States of America must be acknowledged, even, for example, to the degree that parochial leadership attends these celebrations.[9]

3. Realize that language is often nonverbal and also connected to identity. Given the high rate of English-language acquisition by second-generation Hispanic immigrants and even by their immigrant parents, non-Spanish-speaking pastoral workers sometimes wonder whether it is really necessary that they learn Spanish to work with this population.[10] The use of Spanish, although called for less frequently than if they were in Mexico, is important because it sends the message that the language is worth learning. Later generations are ashamed, at times, of a language that is seemingly only spoken by the lower class since, in many places, most manual labor is carried out by native Spanish speakers. Furthermore, by affirming the language the pastoral worker affirms the family of origin. Finally, in relation to nonverbal language, those who are not native to the culture should keep in mind that much is communicated without words. Careful attention to body language, as when certain gestures such as a hug or a kiss are appropriate, goes a long way in respecting the culture. A helpful strategy in getting to know the culture is to continually consult someone well versed in it. It is okay to ask!

4. Be careful about preaching or teaching only in Spanish. A common practice in many parishes is to have Masses only in Spanish, despite the fact that many of the children and young people present predominantly speak English among themselves. Catechesis, similarly, is sometimes only done in Spanish. Among the reasons given for adhering to this practice are that this way the parents will be able to help train their children in matters of the faith (assuming that their parents have not mastered English). Also, the children, who quickly pick up English, can nonetheless retain their ability to use Spanish if that is what they hear in church settings. The Spanish language is, for many Hispanics, a language of the heart because they learned it at home and English is more of the head because they learned or perfected it in school.

The fact remains, however, that it is typical for the second generation to identity more with the country in which they were born than with that of their parents. Therefore, they will definitely speak more English, the language of much of their mental constructs. Often they do not understand many of the words that are used in Spanish Masses; in that situation a few words spoken in English go a long way to help them find meaning in the liturgy. The same can be said for catechesis, particularly at a time when bilingual textbooks are now available. In this way the parents can also become involved. Likewise, what happens when they get older and because their theological language is in Spanish they are not able to explain or make sense of it in English? It is hard enough, when the medium is English, to attempt to respond to adult faith questions with childhood catechism answers, but to do it when Spanish is involved? Quite a challenge! Is it any wonder that Mexican-Americans as well as other Hispanics often look outside the Church for faith formation of some sort?

5. In the Mexican cultures, as in most Latino ones, relationality is given great importance. Do not ignore this fact! Baptismal godparents, for example, are not only expected to have a special relationship with the child they have sponsored for baptism, but are related to the parents of the child as *compadres.* This *compadrazo,* sometimes translated as "godparentage," "usually involves a solemn commitment to the family as friend, confidant and advisor—and a commitment to become a true 'other parent' to the newly baptized child."[11] Other celebrations at key life moments (sometimes called "rites of passage") such as maturity, commitment, and even death, accent the importance of belonging.[12] As previously noted, it is not uncommon for friends and family to help cover some of the expenses for these major celebrations.

The importance of the parish organizing home visits, for example, around the Advent popular custom, the *posadas,* cannot be overstated. An arrangement whereby different families take charge of hosting the *posada* over the nine-day period stresses this key relationality component. Good hospitality builds good friendships! Don't be afraid to visit in other settings as well. Catholic immigrants are often touched by a visit from parish representatives since other religious groups and denominations have already visited them and invited them to become part of their churches. Home visits also remind pastoral agents that they do not have to be in charge of every religious encounter—in such visits, they meet people on their own turf.

Similarly, personal invitations on the part of parish leadership are needed before persons become more active in ministries such as religious education, extraordinary Eucharistic minister, lector, cantor, social justice, and so on. This personal touch is infinitely more successful than are general calls made from the pulpit or in the Sunday bulletin. Time taken to discern and personally invite natural leaders from the Mexican community to such important bodies as the parish council will yield a hundredfold results, provided these relationships are sincere and sustained.

6. Keep in mind that recently arrived Mexicans, like other immigrant groups, need their own liturgical and social time together. For people whose way of life has changed radically in a relatively short period of time—those who find their new type of work, social ambiance, language, and legal system entirely foreign—the opportunity to worship in their own language and with their own traditional symbols and hymns is a real grace. Despite whatever alienation we are feeling, religious practice should provide a place where we can once again feel at home in the universe through our encounters with God and community.[13] Previously in the history of the U.S. Catholic Church, ethnic or national parishes provided such welcome havens for the immigrants, although the practice is uncommon today.[14] Against the grain of the current "We're in America and so they have to assimilate!" mentality, it may be time to revisit this pastoral model, which, to a large extent, was very successful in eventually helping the immigrant to integrate into the U.S. Church and society. These parishes, although not officially designated as such, exist for the Mexican community in the United States of America. Yet, given the numbers, their members are now living in other sectors where the reality is more multicultural.[15] Are bilingual or multilingual liturgies the answer? Not necessarily. Although many parishes have found that occasional ones can be an expression and a stimulus for unity among the different racial and ethnic communities (such as at Pentecost or on the patronal feast of the parish), for the reasons given above, immigrant groups regularly need their own space where they are fed liturgically so that when they gather with the larger community, they bring their own strengths and charisms for the service of all. A helpful liturgical reality to keep in mind here is the importance of gesture. For example, during multicultural liturgies, some parishes incorporate nonverbal reverential gestures done by representatives of the different communities such as foot washing, flag- or banner-carrying, or preparation of the baptismal font or the Eucharistic table—all done to communicate a sense of unity amid diversity. These gestures, as with the use of simple sacred music in different languages, do not require a great deal of knowledge of specific languages. It is especially in liturgy that "actions speak louder than words."

7. Children and young people are a great resource for bridging cultural barriers. Because they are often bilingual, with a foot in each cultural world, young persons should occasionally be called upon to serve as lectors, cantors, ministers of hospitality, and the like. In a sense, children are big "uniters" because they make friends quickly, helping to create a friendlier environment where adults can also feel at ease. At a party, for example, parents are often happy to see their children link up with other children there, thus helping to create a warmer atmosphere. Immigrant families with children seem to assimilate more easily into U.S. patterns of life. Along the same lines, if the parish wishes to involve immigrants, especially young Mexican couples who often have small children, it is important to provide either activities that the whole family can participate in, such as picnics, or child care during the activity. When parents first come into the country, it is difficult to find child care or sitters. Be aware, though, that newer immigrants may prefer to keep their children with them than to leave them with a total stranger.

8. Pay attention to the environment. Mexicans come from a country where great attention is paid to decoration. Both their indigenous and Spanish ancestors made great religious use of architecture, color, music, dance, and symbol. Especially during the Baroque period, known for its artistic exuberance and when many Mexican colonial churches were built, the missionaries used this type of art to explain the mysteries of the faith. In their evangelization, they engaged drama, music, and the visual arts.[16] This Latin American tradition of the connection between arts and worship, versus a Northern European more Protestant, iconoclastic one, is one of the reasons why Mexicans and other Latinos in the United States of America often do not feel at home in what seems to be to them a more Protestant worship space. Pastoral teams, therefore, might think twice about discouraging the kind of elaborate decoration and physical preparation that is part of any large celebration, especially that of Our Lady of Guadalupe, Christmas, or Holy Week. These visual preparations and manifestations play a major role in community catechesis and group identity, to say nothing of the subsequent connection to social justice. A young priest in Las Cruces, New Mexico, for example, described the validation and joy Hispanics in the parish felt when, as part of the worship space's renovation, the image of Our Lady of Guadalupe was moved from the vestibule to the sanctuary. If your Mother is being respected, so are you. This transfer is reminiscent of African-Americans no longer having to sit in the back of the bus.

A similar need to pay attention to the tactile and visual, especially in the religiously symbolic arena was noted by María Elena Cardeña, a lay campus minister in La Verne, California. In her work with Latino college students, Cardeña found that students responded enthusiastically to such Mexican symbols as Guadalupe, the Chicano eagle used by the United Farm Workers, and Emiliano Zapata, the early twentieth-century Mexican Revolutionary leader. She speaks of a profound spirituality among the students whose faith journey can be nourished by biblical symbols such as the eagle imagery in Isaiah or passages speaking of solidarity with one's people. Other prominent symbols, which do not necessarily require use within a Eucharistic liturgy, are the distribution of ashes and holy cards. "On a campus, you do not necessarily have to gather people in order to minister to them as they go about their busy day."[17]

What gets in the way of reaching out to an immigrant Mexican population?

There are several factors that make Mexicans, along with other Hispanics, feel unwelcome in the Catholic Church, and therefore, more likely to join other Christian denominations or religious groups. As the U.S. Bishops' Committee on Hispanic Affairs reported in 1999:

> Among these factors are excessive administrative tasks and rules in Catholic parishes, which often override a spontaneous, personal, and warm reception. For example, some Hispanics complain about having to fill out complicated forms and produce evidence of being registered, such as showing contribution envelopes, before they can receive the sacraments. In contrast, evangelical churches conduct home visits, provide powerful preaching that skillfully links Scripture with everyday life, and foster a notion of Church as extended family that provides Hispanics with a sense of belonging to God's family.[18]

Parishes that take the time to welcome newcomers through home visits generally have been more successful in drawing them into their faith communities.

Isn't there a point at which we should stop providing special pastoral care to Mexican immigrants so that they will assimilate into U.S. culture like the rest of Catholics in this country?

Several researchers are now questioning the value of promoting assimilation at all costs because of the psychological stress often connected with it.[19] Although this type of stress is not necessarily negative, in that it can also be a positive creative force such as when an individual masters a new language and experiences a greater acceptance, recent findings demonstrate that immigrants who acculturate too much or too little are at most risk psychologically. In examining the process of acculturation, a type of assimilation that has to do with the process of a person taking on another culture, we see in John W. Berry and Uichol Kim's categories realistic groupings, at the risk of oversimplification, of the various ways in which immigrants respond to the new culture. These categories or modes of acculturation, which they identify as *assimilation, integration, separation,* and *marginalization,* deal with two central issues: (1) "Is my cultural identity of value and to be retained?" and (2) "Are positive relations with the larger (dominant) society to be sought?"[20]

In the first mode, *assimilation,* an immigrant relinquishes her or his cultural identity so as to be part of the larger, dominant society. An example of this mode for Mexican-Americans would be to simply to start to see themselves as regular "Americans," who attempt to sever linguistic and cultural ties with the native culture. This attitude is reflected in what a Mexican-American uncle told his nephew: "It's all right to be a Chicano (Mexican-American) as long as you don't act like one."

In contrast, the second mode, *integration,* "implies the maintenance of cultural integrity as well as the movement to become an integral part of a larger societal framework."[21] Bilingualism and biculturalism as goals to be maintained embody this type of approach. The native culture is seen as something valuable and therefore something to pass on to the next generation. This mode embraces the cultural mosaic model, unity amid diversity.

The third, *separation,* is marked by a self-imposed withdrawal from the larger society. Some of the Mexican immigrants who demonstrate this mode are those who refuse to learn English and insist that they are creating "otro México" (another Mexico) here in the United States of America. Berry and Kim, however, add that at times, as when it is exercised, not only by the immigrant group but by the larger society, this separation can become racist, as in the case of segregation or apartheid. Some older Mexican-Americans still recall the days when there were signs in restaurants in the Southwest that said "No Mexicans allowed."

Finally, the fourth category, *marginalization*, "is accompanied by a good deal of collective and individual confusion and anxiety. It is characterized by having lost essential features of one's culture, but not having replaced them by entering the larger society."[22] Perhaps some examples of this mode may be those who speak neither Spanish nor English well, feel a connectedness to neither the United States of America nor Mexico, and therefore see themselves solely as victims of both societies. The authors caution: "This is not to say that such groups have no culture, but to claim only that this culture may be disorganized and may not be supportive of the individual and his or her needs during the process of acculturation."[23] One wonders whether youth gang culture among Mexican-Americans, to the extent that it is destructive to the persons involved, fits this description.

One of the most surprising findings of recent research demonstrates that Latino immigrants are often more hopeful, and, therefore, more inclined to experience better mental health than later generations of U.S.-born Latinas or Latinos. While the immigrants generally have less income and education, their reference group is different. "Whereas new immigrants may make positive social comparisons to their country of origin counterparts, second-generation and later generation Latinos may make negative social comparisons to mainstream American society because of the different ways that prejudice, discrimination, and devalued ethnic minority status limit their once optimistic aspirations."[24]

While recent adult immigrants have a sense of themselves in terms of identity and self-image, Mexican-American children and descendents of the first generation often do not. Thus, in a way, despite the struggles with language, immigrants are easier to work with because they take advantage of what is offered to them. Non-Hispanic pastoral agents get to practice their Spanish with them and do corporal works of mercy. Is it any wonder that the majority of Hispanic ministry in the United States of America is really ministry with recently arrived immigrants? While in many ways they are the ones who most need the help, more assimilated Mexican-Americans cannot be ignored as they often suffer from more of an anthropological poverty, that is, one that does not allow them to love and embrace the person that God made them. This graced self-identity and affirmation will go a long way in helping them to be "bridge people" between the very persons who desperately need each other in terms of God's plan of salvation at both ends of the economic scale.

What are some misconceptions surrounding Mexican-Americans?

One of the major misconceptions is that there is no difference between them and newly arrived immigrants from Mexico. People frequently assume that Mexican-Americans will speak Spanish and if they do not, they are often made to feel inferior for not doing so. When a Mexican-American couple was asked in public to say the "Hail Mary" in Spanish in a Midwest church, the assumption that they would speak Spanish, much less know the prayer in Spanish, proved to be embarrassing for them and their children.

If Mexican-Americans embrace certain U.S. cultural values, they are said to be "losing their culture"—as if cultures are not dynamic and in constant flux. It is important to keep in mind that cultural behaviors, like language, become part of a person's repertoire. In other words, bicultural persons grow up knowing when certain behaviors are appropriate, given the cultural context, and when they are not. Also, the contact of cultures produces newer ones. It is not a question of whether one is more "A" or "B"; perhaps one has now become "C."

In the area of ministry among Mexican-American youth this lack of appreciation for the dynamic quality of culture is of special concern to those relatively few persons writing in the field. One of the most difficult aspects of understanding the reality of these youth—together with designing and implementing ministerial programs—is the fact that this diverse population is a type of moving target. Second-generation American Hispanics grow up in a country different from that of their parents, and the environment in which they grow up is different from the environment that nurtured their parents. Yet, to ignore what is known to constitute 50 percent of the Hispanic population (the number under the age of twenty-six, with more than 33 percent being under the age of eighteen) is unconscionable.[25] Recent writings, some of which are based on current research with young Catholics, are starting to address this complexity and recommend new pastoral strategies.[26]

What are some areas where differences in values and cultural perceptions can be conflictive or problematic between Mexicans, Mexican-Americans, and U.S. mainstream society?

1. Time: U.S. mainstream culture values promptness while, in general, Latino culture is more laid back. It is not uncommon to have the church be almost empty when it is time for the Mass to begin and then gradually fill up as it continues. Once they are there, however, Latinos are not in a hurry to leave and goodbyes in the parking lot can be seemingly endless—a behavior that does not promote harmony with the Euro-Americans coming to the next Mass! "The Hispanic nature is not to follow the clock. To the Anglo 'time is money' and the clock 'runs,' but to the Hispanic 'time is life' and the clock 'walks.' However, in the American business world they realize the importance of following the clock and adjust their habits to keep a place in the work force."[27]

2. Family: While U.S. culture often defines family in terms of the nuclear family consisting of Mother, Father, and children, Mexicans, as do many traditional cultures, understand family in more extended terms, mainly, nuclear family plus grandparents, aunts and uncles, cousins, nieces, nephews, and the like. Elders are afforded special respect. Their names are often prefaced with the title "Don" or "Doña." Some persons who are not related by blood or by marriage are still seen as being part of the family. This notion of extended family brings with it a certain responsibility. It is not uncommon, for example, for uncles and aunts to help bring their nieces and nephews to live in the States. Older brothers and sisters are expected to help take care of their younger siblings, even sometimes to the point of putting them through school. Situations involving other financial or emotional difficulties, including sickness, advanced age, and unemployment, are occasions to lean on one's family for help. Many immigrant families, for example, often live together under one roof until they are able to establish themselves on their own. This accountability to family is also expected when making major decisions such as choosing a marriage partner or vocation or changing denominations or religions. At times, it can be a source of great tension, particularly when the family is not in agreement with the individual's decision. Perhaps this is a case where, in order to grow in compassion and openness, individual cultures needed to be stretched to become more communal, while more communal ones need to pay more attention to the individual.

Another source of great tension is the existence of *machismo,* or an attitude of male dominance. While much less so than before, some Mexican men feel that it is solely up to the woman to take care of the children and perform household chores. In terms of decision making, they see themselves as the ones "who wear the pants" and therefore have the final word. An increasing number of women working outside of the home and a general societal shift away from destructive attitudes that view women as subservient are helping families move toward equality and mutuality.

3. Education: Contrary to what some perceive, education is an important value for Hispanics. It is not necessarily the same as formal academic education. In Spanish, an "educated person," or *persona educada,* implies a person with good manners and respect for self and authority. Because Mexican immigrants often do not have good formal education and they experience how the lack of it hinders their rise up the social economic ladder, they try to impress upon their children its importance. This aspiration, however, does not always translate into educational achievement. As reported in chapter 2, in 2002 the rate of graduation from high school for the general Hispanic population was still a very low 57 percent compared with 88.7 percent for the general U.S. population. Aside from the innumerable problems around the lack of English-language competency, many Hispanic parents do not understand the intricacies of navigating the educational system. Translators, bilingual teachers, and a climate sensitive to their needs, such as in situations where the children migrate to different parts of the country year round working in the harvests, are invaluable. "To fully engage Hispanic audiences in the learning process, particular attention should be given to gaining and maintaining trust."[28]

Parents need to be encouraged to also take advantage of English classes, community colleges, and the like in furthering their own education and thus setting a good example for their children. In the area of religious education it is encouraging to see that Hispanics make up more than 25 percent of all Catholics in formation programs.[29] The number of Hispanics in formal higher education theological degree programs, however, is quite low, largely due to not having the necessary background to get into them.[30] There is a constant request therefore among these Latino communities for Spanish-speaking priests.

Doesn't much of the solution to the problem of a shortage of priests lie in bringing in priests from Latin American countries where they have an abundance of vocations?

Although some dioceses in the United States of America continue to rely on Mexico and Latin America for priestly vocations, to say nothing of the many Latin American women and men religious who are working in the United States of America, this approach is much more shortsighted than it seems. Some question the U.S. Church for participating in the global brain drain that is increasingly drawing more human resources to richer countries. As a result, the United States of America has more priests at its service than most other countries throughout the world (with the exception of Europe), especially among the poorer ones.[31] Other U.S. Catholics, among them even Mexican-American Catholics, voice concerns that their international pastors do not understand them. Whatever the case, the numbers show an increasing reliance on foreign priests; therefore, cultural orientation programs and seminary training for those who come in their earlier years are of great importance.[32]

Pastoral Principles to Further Develop Hispanic Ministry

By way of summary, Alejandro Aguilera-Titus, associate director of the Secretariat for Hispanic Affairs of the U.S. Conference of Catholic Bishops, provides some essential pastoral principles to further develop Hispanic ministry. "The principles follow a developmental sequence that brings Hispanic Catholics, and other groups, from new comers to stewards of the faith community. It also transforms parishes into missionary and evangelizing faith communities that embrace all the baptized in their God given human diversity."[33]

1. Meet the people where they are. Hispanic Catholics rejoice when other Catholics visit them with good news, affirm their gifts, and invite them to the faith community to be at home away from home.
2. Make people feel at home. Hispanics feel welcomed when they have room to be themselves and to strengthen their own sense of identity as they adapt to a different culture from a position of strength.
3. Develop ministries and ministers. Hispanics are empowered when parish staff and leaders of the community work with them to develop and provide a comprehensive Hispanic ministry that includes the four dimensions of Christian life modeled in the first Christian communities (Acts 2:42–47) and included in *Encuentro & Mission* (i.e., formation, missionary aspect, communion in mission, liturgy, and prayer life).
4. Build relationships across cultures and ministries. Hispanics are willing to share their stories, celebrate together, and build relationships between Hispanics

from different countries of origin and with the other communities and ministries of the parish.

5. Champion leadership development and formation. Hispanic leaders are eager to learn and seek opportunities for ongoing faith formation and training for ministry, including certificate and degree programs that are accessible.

6. View and manage crisis as opportunities for growth. Hispanics who have developed a sense of belonging to a parish seek more meaningful ways to be involved in the life of the faith community and for the parish to be more involved in the life of their families and communities.

7. Open wide the doors to the decision-making process. Hispanics want to have a space at the table where decisions are made on the life and direction of Hispanic ministry and of the faith community as a whole. This includes having a space in the parish council, the parish staff, and other decision groups.

8. Sow and reap full ownership and stewardship. As disciples of Christ, Hispanics seek to contribute time, talent, and treasure to build a culturally diverse faith community that is their own—a community of faith in which all cultures are constantly transformed by gospel values in order to be leaven for the reign of God in society.

Chapter 7

HOW CAN I LEARN MORE ABOUT MEXICAN AND MEXICAN-AMERICAN CATHOLICS?

GENERAL REFERENCES

Because more specific references appear in the notes, the purpose of this chapter is to provide a list of general works and reference material for further consultation in the various areas outlined below and not to relist them all.

Books and Periodicals

Mexican History

Meyer, Michael C., William L. Sherman, and Susan M. Deeds. *The Course of Mexican History.* 7th ed. New York: Oxford University Press, 2003.

History of Mexican-Americans

Dolan, Jay P., and Gilberto M. Hinojosa, eds. *Mexican Americans and the Catholic Church, 1900–1965.* Notre Dame, IN: University of Notre Dame Press, 1994.

González, Manuel G. *Mexicanos: A History of Mexicans in the United States.* Bloomington and Indianapolis: Indiana University Press, 1999.

Religion and Sociology

Espinosa, Gastón, Virgilio Elizondo, and Jesse Mirana, eds. *Latino Religions and Civic Activism in the United States.* New York: Oxford University Press, 2005.

U.S. Hispanic Theology

Aquino, María Pilar, Daisy L. Machado, and Jeanette Rodríguez, eds. *A Reader in Latina Feminist Theology: Religion and Justice.* Austin: University of Texas Press, 2002.

Bañuelas, Arturo J., ed. *Mestizo Christianity: Theology from the Latino Perspective.* Maryknoll, NY: Orbis Books, 1995.

Díaz, Miguel H. *On Being Human: U.S. Hispanic and Rahnerian Perspectives.* Maryknoll, NY: Orbis Books, 2001.

Fernández, Eduardo C. *La Cosecha: Harvesting Contemporary United States Hispanic Theology (1972–1998).* Collegeville, MN: A Michael Glazier Book, The Liturgical Press, 2000.

Linguistics

Santamaría, Francisco J. *Diccionario de Mejicanismos.* México: Editorial Porrúa, 2005.

Mental Health

Velásquez, Roberto J., Leticia M. Arellano, and Brian W. McNeill, eds. *The Handbook of Chicana/o Psychology* and Mental Health. Mahwah, NJ: Erlbaum Associates, 2004.

Periodical

¡En Marcha! Published by the Secretariat for Hispanic Affairs of the U.S. Conference of Catholic Bishops, 3211 4th St. NE, Washington, DC 20017.

Pastoral Resources

Davis, Kenneth G., OFM, conv., ed. and comp. *Misa, Mesa y Musa: Liturgy in the U.S. Hispanic Church*. Schiller Park, IL: World Library Publications, 1997.

_____, and Jorge L. Presmanes, OP, eds. *Preaching and Culture in Latino Congregations*. Chicago: Liturgical Training Publications, 2000.

_____, and Leopoldo Pérez, OMI, eds. *Preaching the Teaching: Hispanics, Homiletics, and Catholic Social Justice Doctrine*. Scranton: University of Scranton Press, 2005.

Empereur, James, and Eduardo C. Fernández. *La Vida Sacra: Contemporary Hispanic Sacramental Theology*. Lanham, MD: Rowman & Littlefield, 2006.

Mexican American Cultural Center (MACC). *Quinceañera: Celebración de la Vida, Guia Para Los Que Presiden el Rito Religioso/Quinceañera: Guidebook for the Presider of the Religious Rite*. San Antonio: Mexican American Cultural Center, 1999.

Pérez-Rodríguez, Arturo, and and Mark Francis. *Primero Dios: Hispanic Liturgical Resource*. Chicago: Liturgy Training Publications, 1997.

Books in Spanish for Education and Training

Codina, Victor. *Sacramentos de la Vida* [Sacraments of Life]. México: Ediciones Dabar, 1993.

Saravia, Javier. *Leyendo Los Signos de Los Tiempos: Herramientas de Análisis Social y Cultural* [Reading the Signs of the Times: Tools for Social and Cultural Analysis]. México: Obra Nacional de la Buena Prensa, A.C., 1999.

_____. *La Religiosidad Popular, Extranjera en Su Propia Tierra* [Popular Religiosity: A Stranger in Her Own Land]. México: Obra Nacional de la Buena Prensa, A.C., 2000.

_____. *La Solidaridad con los Migrantes en la Vida y en la Biblia* [Solidarity with Migrants in Life and in the Bible]. México: Obra Nacional de la Buena Prensa, A.C., 2004.

Internet Site

Bookstores and Other Pastoral Materials

Many of the resources in this section include music.

Claretian Press Hispanic Ministry. Contains the Hispanic Ministry Resource Center, which offers numerous resources, many bilingual.
http://hmrc.claretianpubs.org/

Liguori Bookstore. Also carries books in Spanish.
http://www.liguori.org/

Liturgy Training Publications. Excellent source for liturgical texts and liturgy-related items, with books in Spanish.
http://www.ltp.org/index.html

Oregon Catholic Press. Publishes music, worship materials, and books, with materials in Spanish and Vietnamese.
http://www.ocp.org/en/

Spanish Speaking Bookstore—Chicago. Specializes in religious titles in Spanish, both trade and public.
(773) 878-2117
http://www.centerstage.net/literature/bookstores/spanish-speaking.html

World Library Publications. Online bookstore and purveyor of Church music, some in Spanish.
http://www.wlp.jspaluch.com/wlp/

Catholic Church

Los Angeles archdiocesan website. In Spanish.
http://www.archdiocese.la/espanol/index.php

Pax Catholic Communication. A service of the archdiocese of Miami with the unique mission of evangelizing and proclaiming the good news through the media.
http://www.paxcc.org/

Tu Compañero Católico. A Spanish-language Catholic radio program. The half-hour show airs weekly on seventy-two stations across the United Sates of America.
www.nccbuscc.org/ccc/tcc.shtml

U.S. Conference of Catholic Bishops, Secretariat for Hispanic Affairs. Among the most helpful of sites.
www.usccb.org/hispanicaffairs

Christmas Customs

Navidad Latina. In Spanish. Has Christmas customs throughout Latin America.
http://www.navidadlatina.com/tradiciones/welcome.asp

Day of the Dead

Día de los Muertos. Much helpful information about the celebration; includes tasty recipes!
http://www.azcentral.com/ent/dead/food/

Education

Academy of Catholic Hispanic Theologians in the U.S. (ACHTUS)
http://www.achtus.org/

La Asociación para la Educación Teológica Hispana. Ecumenical site. Many resources in Spanish, especially pertaining to the Bible.
http://www.aeth.org/

University of San Diego Center for the Study of Latino Catholicism. Incredible number of helpful links.
http://www.sandiego.edu/theo/Latino-Cath/

Immigration and Migration

Catholic Migrant Workers. Gives information about the movements, events, and issues. Well-organized. Also contains personal stories and some songs.
http://www.cmfn.org/index.html

Justice for Immigration: The Catholic Campaign for Immigration Reform. Provides much-needed information, including the Church's position, in both Spanish and English, to address this pressing issue.
www.justiceforimmigrants.org

Liturgy

Instituto Nacional Hispano de Liturgia. Bilingual site for the national Hispanic liturgy organization, which has done much to train persons and provide materials in the area of liturgy.

http://liturgia.cua.edu/about/

Pastoral Training Centers

Mexican American Cultural Center in San Antonio, Texas. One of the most famous of these centers; includes access to their bookstore.

http://www.maccsa.org/

Priests

Asociación National de Sacerdotes Hispanos. The site for the National Association of Hispanic priests in the U.S. in Spanish. Helpful links.

http://www.ansh.org/index.htm

Catechesis

Catequésis y Liturgia. Part of the site for the Diocese of San Jose, California. Contains the Hispanic Ministry newsletter by Lupita C. Vital; all the articles are in Spanish.

http://www.dsj.org/educate/catechetics.asp?id=4

Youth Ministry Formation

Instituto Fe y Vida, Institute for Faith and Life. Located in Stockton, California, but has a national outreach; dedicated to empowering young people for leadership in church and society. Site has a Spanish section. Significant offering of resources and results of research.

http://www.feyvida.org/contact.html

Videos and DVDs

Immigration and Migration

Dying to Live: A Migrant's Journey. DVD. Groody River Films. Chicago, 2005. 33 minutes. Available at www.nd.edu/~latino/units/clsc.htm.

Entre Sueños y Fronteras: Historias detrás de la Controversia sobre la Inmigración. Video. Maryknoll World Productions. Maryknoll, NY. 56 minutes. Available at 1-800-227-8523.

La Gran Posada: A Christmas Celebration. Video. Family Theater Productions. Hollywood, CA. 57 minutes. Available at 1-800-299-7729.

Posada: A Night to Cross all Borders. DVD. Loyola Productions. Los Angeles, 2007. 57 minutes. Available at www.loyolaproductions.com.

Liturgy and Popular Piety

Alma del Pueblo/Soul of the City. Video. JM Communications. Houston. 28 minutes. Available at 713-524-1382; http://www.jmcommunications.com.

¡Fiesta! Celebrations at San Fernando by Thomas A. Kane. Video. Paulist Press, 1999. 49 minutes. English- and Spanish-language versions available. Available at www.paulistpress.com.

Liturgical Training Publications. Video. Chicago, 1999. 15-minute presentations designed to accompany Francis and Pérez-Rodríguez's *Primero Dios* (see above), entitled: *Un Pueblo Sacramental/A Sacramental People.* Includes six 15-minute segments, available in Spanish or English: (1) Introduction, (2) First Communion, (3) Presentation of the Child, (4) Quince Años,

(5) Wedding, (6) Mourning the Dead. Available at 1-800-933-1800.

Our Lady of Guadalupe

Juan Diego: Mensajero de Guadalupe. Video. Animation, in Spanish. 30 minutes. Orbis. Available at 1-800-935-2222.

General Reference Work

Davis, Kenneth G., Eduardo C. Fernández, and Veronica Méndez, eds. *United States Hispanic Catholics Trends and Works, 1990–2000.* Scranton: University of Scranton Press, 2002.

NOTES

Preface

1. Eduardo Porter and Elisabeth Malkin, "Way North of the Border," *New York Times,* September 30, 2005.

2. Most of the proverbs used for the opening of chapters have been taken from *Refranes: Southwestern Spanish Proverbs,* comp. and trans. Rubén Cobos (Sante Fe: Museum of New Mexico Press, 1985).

3. Ibid., vii.

Chapter 1

1. Ignacio Bernal, "The Pre-Columbian Era," in *A Compact History of Mexico,* ed. Daniel Cosío Villegas (México: Colegio de México, 2002), 23.

2. Bernal Díaz del Castillo as quoted in Ignacio Bernal, "The End of the Indian World," in *A Compact History of Mexico,* ed. Daniel Cosío Villegas (México: Colegio de México, 2002), 37.

3. For a scholarly treatment of one of the great prophets at the time of the early Spanish conquest and evangelization, see Gustavo Gutiérrez, *Las Casas: In Search of the Poor of Jesus Christ,* trans. Robert R. Barr (Maryknoll, NY: Orbis Books, 1993).

4. Manuel G. Gonzáles, *Mexicanos: A History of Mexicans in the United States* (Bloomington and Indianapolis: Indiana University Press, 1999), 25.

5. The historicity of the apparitions to the Indian (now St.) Juan Diego, especially in recent times around his beatification and canonization, has been hotly debated. I provide some references in chapter 4 for those who wish to pursue the topic at greater length.

6. On the topic of the early evangelization of Mexico, I highly recommend Robert Ricard's classic work, *The Spiritual Conquest*

of Mexico: An Essay on the Apostolate and the Evangelizing Methods of the Mendicant Orders in New Spain: 1523–1572, trans. Lesley Bird Simpson (Berkeley: University of California Press, 1988).

7. By "inculturation" here I mean the adaptation of the divine message to the reality of the people or, as I have heard Rosa María Icaza, CCVI, describe it, "preaching the Gospel in a way people can understand." I am indebted to Fray Gonzalo Balderas, OP, for helping me to distinguish the various missological strategies which are summarized in the section.

8. For a scholarly work, beautifully illustrated, on the relationship between liturgy and architecture in Mexico's early evangelization, see Jaime Lara's *City, Temple, Stage: Eschatological Architecture and Liturgical Theatrics in New Spain* (Notre Dame, IN: University of Notre Dame Press, 2004).

9. Alejandra Moreno Toscana, "The Spiritual Conquest," in *A Compact History of Mexico,* ed. Daniel Cosío Villegas (México: Colegio de México, 2002), 56.

10. Luis González, "The Century of Enlightment," in *A Compact History of Mexico,* ed. Daniel Cosío Villegas (México: Colegio de México, 2002), 72.

11. Ibid.

12. During the nineteenth century, Catholicism under Pope Pius IX underwent a reactionary phase, one characterized by a refusal to accept the modern ideas of the freedom of religion, the freedom of the press, and the importance of the separation of church and state. See E. Fernández, *La Cosecha: Harvesting Contemporary United States Hispanic Theology (1972–1998)* (Collegeville, MN: The Liturgical Press, 2000), 102.

Chapter 2

1. The popular song composed by Alberto Cortéz bears the same name as the phrase quoted.

2. The 1997 movie, distributed by Warner Brothers Studio, was written and directed by Gregory Nava and produced by

Moctezuma Esparza. I am indebted to Fray Ponchie Vasquez, OFM, for both the suggestion and the transcript of this scene.

3. While the majority of Hispanics live in the western or southern parts of the country, recent reports from the U.S. Census Bureau show that some counties in nontraditional Hispanic states such as Georgia and North Carolina now have sizable Hispanic populations. "Hispanics within some counties in North Carolina, Georgia, Iowa, Arkansas, Minnesota, and Nebraska represented between 6.0 percent and 24.9 percent of the county's total population...The largest Mexican populations lived in counties that had large Hispanic populations, including Los Angeles County, California (3.0 million), Harris County, Texas (815,000), and Cook County, Illinois (786,000)." Betsy Guzmán, *The Hispanic Population: Census 2000 Brief*, C2KBR/01-3 (Washington, DC: U.S. Census Bureau, May 2001), 5.

4. Much of this chapter is an updating and refocusing of chapter 1, "Hispanics in the American Catholic Church and Culture," in my book, *La Cosecha: Harvesting Contemporary United States Hispanic Theology (1972–1998)* (Collegeville, MN: The Liturgical Press, 2000).

5. Manuel G. González, *Mexicanos: A History of Mexicans in the United States* (Bloomington and Indianapolis: Indiana University Press, 1999). His first three chapters cover periods before 1848.

6. For an eyewitness description of mission life in seventeenth-century colonial New Mexico, see an excerpt of Fray Alonso de Benavides's writing found in *Cross and Sword: An Eyewitness History of Christianity and Latin America*, ed. H. McKennie Goodpastor (Maryknoll, NY: Orbis Books, 1989), 57–58. For a more systematic treatment of the same during that and the following centuries, especially in terms of art, folklore, and the role of religion in daily life, see Luciano C. Hendren, "Daily Life on the Frontier," in *Fronteras: A History of the Latin American Church in the USA Since 1513*, ed. Moises Sandoval (San Antonio, TX: MACC, 1983), 103–39. *On the Rim of Christendom: A Biography of Eusebio Francisco Kino, Pacific Coast Pioneer* by Herbert Eugene Bolton (New York: Macmillan Company, 1936) is a

moving account of the work of the famed Jesuit missionary, much beloved, even to the present day. For an extensive, annotated collection of original documents concerning the history of Catholic Hispanics, see *¡Presente!: U.S. Latino Catholics from Colonial Origins to the Present,* ed. Timothy Matovina and Gerald E. Poyo (Maryknoll, NY: Orbis Books, 2000).

7. Issued by the U.S. Conference of Catholic Bishops in 1987 (Washington, DC: USCC).

8. Ibid., 4.

9. See R. Acuña's *Occupied America: A History of Chicanos* (New York: HarperCollins Publishers, 1988).

10. Manuel Espinoza, *Crusaders of the Río Grande* (Chicago, IL: Institute of Jesuit History, 1942), 365.

11. Acuña, *Occupied America.*

12. Stated at Mobile Jesuit conference in June 1992.

13. M. Sandoval, *On the Move: A History of the Hispanic Church in the United States* (Maryknoll, NY: Orbis Books, 1990), 30.

14. In *Prophets Denied Honor: An Anthology on the Hispanic American Church in the United States,* ed. A. M. Stevens-Arroyo (Maryknoll, NY: Orbis Books, 1980), 79.

15. Ibid.

16. Ibid., 31. See Lynn Bridgers, *Death's Deceiver: The Life of Joseph P. Machebeuf* (Albuquerque: University of New Mexico Press, 1997).

17. Among the most important of these leaders was the famed "Cura de Taos," Padre A. J. Martínez, a New Mexican priest active in education, publishing, and politics. His difficulties with Archbishop Lamy are the subject of many works. See *Reluctant Dawn: Historia del Padre A. J. Martínez, Cura de Taos* (San Antonio: Mexican American Cultural Center, 1976) by Juan Romero with Moises Sandoval. Also, *Padre Martínez and Bishop Lamy* (Las Vegas, NM: The Pan-American Publishing Company, 1978), written by Ray John de Aragon. Archbishop Lamy's renown spread with the publication of *Death Comes for the Archbishop* (New York: Vintage Books, 1971), a novel by Willa

Cather based on his life, and *Lamy of Santa Fe, His Life and Times* (New York: Farrar Straus and Giroux, 1975) by Paul Horgan.

18. Juan Romero, with Sandoval, *Reluctant Dawn*, 40.

19. Ibid. A good example of these native folk traditions is the Penitente movement, a lay confraternity whose origins and practices can be traced back to the penitential societies of medieval Spain. The movement has been quite controversial over the decades. See C. Gilbert Romero's *Hispanic Devotional Piety: Tracing the Biblical Roots* (Maryknoll, NY: Orbis Books, 1991) along with "Saint Makers in the Desert" by Mary Elizabeth and Leon J. Podles in *America*, November 7, 1992. Alberto López Pulido has drawn from oral interviews to tell their story, a witness to the power of penance through charity, prayer, and good example. See his *The Sacred World of the Penitentes* (Washington, DC: Smithsonian Institutional Press, 2000).

20. See M. García's *Desert Immigrants: The Mexicans of El Paso, 1880–1920* (New Haven: Yale University Press, 1981) and Acuña, *Occupied America*. Manuel González reports that "some eight thousand refugees, for example, crossed the border from Piedras Negras, Coahuila, to Eagle Pass, Texas, in a single day in October 1913; and in one week in June 1916, almost five thousand Mexicans poured into El Paso. The numbers increased dramatically, however, once the violence abated." González, *Mexicanos,* 118–19.

21. T. Bokenkotter, *A Concise History of the Catholic Church* (New York: Doubleday Image, 1979), 378.

22. Ibid., 379.

23. Ibid., 378.

24. Ibid., 383.

25. Ibid.

26. Ibid., 396.

27. González, *Mexicanos,* 135–38.

28. González cites a little known statistic discovered by immigration scholar Walter Nugent, mainly, that "some 40 percent of Europeans who migrated to Argentina, Brazil, Canada, and the United States in the half-century before World War I eventually repatriated" (ibid., 135).

29. Ibid., 136.

30. Ibid., 137.

31. Ibid.

32. Various authors provide good historical sources for documenting this era. Among them are two works previously cited, that of M. T. García and R. Acuña. In *El Paso: A Borderlands History* (El Paso: Texas Western Press, 1990), W. H. Timmons describes one of these major guest worker programs, the Bracero program, created by the United States of America in 1942 (242).

33. *Puerto Ricans in the Continental United States: An Uncertain Future,* a report of the U.S. Commission on Civil Rights, October 1976, 18. See A. M. Stevens-Arroyo's treatment of Puerto Rican migration to the mainland during this century in "Puerto Rican Migration to the United States," in *Fronteras,* ed. Moises Sandoval, 269–76, as well as for a perspective from the mainland, A. M. Díaz-Stevens, *Oxcart Catholicism on Fifth Avenue: The Impact of the Puerto Rican Migration upon the Catholic Archdiocese of New York* (Notre Dame, IN: University of Notre Dame Press, 1993). See also *Recognizing the Latino Resurgence in U.S. Religion: The Emmaus Paradigm* by Ana María Díaz-Stevens and Anthony M. Stevens-Arroyo (Boulder, CO: Westview Press, 1998) for a very thorough treatment of Latinos in church and society, told by two persons who have participated intensely in the recent decades' struggle for justice.

34. U.S. Census data, 2005 American Community Survey. See http://factfinder.census.gov/ and search for Dade County, Florida. This report shows that there are eight U.S. cities with immigrant populations of over one million (mostly Hispanic): Chicago, Dallas, Houston, Los Angeles, Miami, New York, San Francisco, and Washington, DC. Most of the Hispanic immigrants are from Mexico.

35. For a concise historical overview of Latinos in the U.S. Church, see Jaime Vidal, "Hispanic Catholics in America," in *The Encyclopedia of American Catholic History,* ed. Michael Glazier and Thomas J. Shelley (Collegeville, MN: The Liturgical Press, 1998), 635–42.

36. The U.S. Population Census is calculated every ten years, the last one having taken place in the year 2000. The U.S. Census Bureau, however, also conducts yearly surveys that shed much light on demographic trends in between the decades. The 2005 American Community Survey from which the most current data are taken is compiled from the yearly surveys.

37. Figures are from Roberto R. Ramírez and G. Patricia de la Cruz, *The Hispanic Population in the United States: March 2002,* Current Population Reports, P20-545 (Washington, DC: U.S. Census Bureau, 2002), 1–2.

38. In a work edited by Rodolfo J. Cortina and Alberto Moncada, *Hispanos en los Estados Unidos,* the point of different histories and different socioeconomic status among the various Hispanic groups is highlighted. The authors decry a lack of social research that takes this large diversity into account. See "El Sentido de la diversidad: recientes investigaciones sobra las minorías en los Estados Unidos," in *Hispanos en los Estados Unidos,* ed. Rodolfo J. Cortina and Alberto Moncada (Madrid: Ediciones de Cultura Hispánica, 1988), 31–58.

39. Guzmán, *The Hispanic Population: Census 2000 Brief,* 2.

40. Ramírez and de la Cruz, *The Hispanic Population in the United States: March 2002,* 3.

41. Guzmán, *The Hispanic Population: Census 2000 Brief,* 7.

42. Ramírez and de la Cruz, *The Hispanic Population in the United States: March 2002,* 3.

43. Ibid., 4.

44. Guzmán, *The Hispanic Population: Census 2000 Brief,* 3. According to the 2005 American Community Survey, Hispanics make up 35.5 percent of the total population of California and Texas.

45. Ramírez and de la Cruz, *The Hispanic Population in the United States: March 2002,* 4.

46. E. Rodríguez, "Realities for Hispanics," *Company* 6 (1988): 9.

47. Ibid.

48. Ramírez and de la Cruz, *The Hispanic Population in the United States: March 2002,* 6.

49. *San Francisco Chronicle,* September 23, 1993.

50. Ramírez and de la Cruz, *The Hispanic Population in the United States: March 2002,* 6.

51. J. G. Fernández, basing herself on the work of J. Moore and R. Pinderhughes *(In the Barrios),* summarizes the history of the term: "Among social scientists and other scholars there is as yet no consensus about the term 'underclass.' During the 60s, urban analysts began to speak of a new dimension to the urban crisis in the form of a large subpopulation of low-income families and individuals whose behavior was different from the general population. In the late 70s and early 80s the underclass were considered an urban group with tendencies of criminal acts, welfare dependency, mental illness, alcoholic, and drug dependency and it included the poorest of the poor." J. G. Fernández, "Latina Garment Workers in El Paso, Texas Challenging the Urban Underclass Model" (unpublished manuscript, MA thesis, University of Texas at El Paso, 1995), 1. See J. Moore and R. Pinderhughes, *In the Barrios* (New York: Russell Sage Foundation, 1993); O. Lewis, *The Children of Sanchez: Autobiography of a Mexican Family* (New York: Vintage Books, 1961); N. Lehmann, "The Origins of the Underclass," *Atlantic Monthly* (June 1986): 31–55, (July 1986): 54–68; and L. M. Mead, "The New Politics of the New Poverty," *The Public Interest* 103 (1991): 3–21. I am indebted to Juanita García Fernández for this discussion of the underclass model as applicable to Latinos in the United States.

52. See D. E. Hayes-Bautista, A. Hurtado, R. Burciaga Valedez, and A. C. R. Hernández, *No Longer a Minority: Latinos and Social Policy in California* (Los Angeles: UCLA Chicano Studies Research Center, 1992), xi. The companion book, published by the same authors and publisher, is *Redefining California: Latino Social Engagement in a Multicultural Society* (Los Angeles: UCLA Chicano Studies Research Center, 1992). While their findings are limited to Latinos in California, the questions they have raised are very significant for studying Latinos in other areas of the country. Hayes-Bautista's most recent book, one in which he continues to debunk the urban underclass model as applied to Latinos in

California, is *La Nueva California: Latinos in the Golden State* (Berkeley: University of California Press, 2004).

53. See González, *Mexicanos,* 237–38.

54. Fernández, "Latina Garment Workers," vi.

55. Ibid.

56. Ibid., 89.

57. Their study is entitled *The Hispanic Catholic in the United States: A Socio-Cultural and Religious Profile* and was published by the Northeast Catholic Pastoral Center for Hispanics, New York, 1985. For a summary of their findings, see especially xi–xiii.

58. Ibid.

59. M. Sandoval, *On the Move.*

60. M. Sandoval, "El Campesino hispano y las iglesias en los Estados Unidos," *Cristianismo y Sociedad* 96 (1988). See also "The Mexican Catholic Community in California" by Jeffrey M. Burns in *Mexican Americans and the Catholic Church, 1900–1965,* ed. Jay P. Dolan and Gilberto M. Hinojosa (Notre Dame, IN: University of Notre Dame Press, 1994), 222–33. This chapter details the impact on the U.S. Catholic Church of both the Cursillo movement and the United Farm Workers, pointing out that Cesar Chávez, its founder, was also a Cursillista.

61. In an address delivered at the Western Vocation Directors Association Convention in 1973, Roger B. Luna, SDB, basing his comments on a survey of Mexican-American priests, gave the following four reasons for the present situation: "(1) The Spanish tradition of not creating a native clergy, (2) open discrimination against Mexicans by priests, (3) taking Mexicans for granted on the part of the church; no special effort to keep them Catholic, and (4) the lack of education, especially higher education, among Mexican young people" (text was printed in *Prophets,* "Why So Few Mexican-American Priests?" 160–63).

62. Y. Tarango, "The Church Struggling to Be Universal: A Mexican American Perspective," *International Review of Mission* 78 (April 1989): 167–73.

63. In a 1988 article in *America* U.S. sociologist and priest Andrew Greeley reported a defection rate of 8 percent among Hispanics during the previous fifteen years—that is nearly one

million Hispanic men and women. See "Defection Among Hispanics," *America,* July 30, 1988, 61–62. In the September 27, 1997 issue of *America,* he repeats the same concern: "One out of five Hispanics who were raised Catholic are no longer Catholic. The church seems unwilling or unable to respond to this cataclysm" (13). See "Defection Among Hispanics (Updated)," 12–13. More recent studies are somewhat more cautious about such conclusions. For example, in the 2003 study entitled "Hispanic Churches in American Public Life," the researchers state: "Although Andrew Greeley noted in 1988 that only 70 percent of all Latinos were Roman Catholic and that this decline was likely to continue over the next twenty-five years, we found that the proportion of Catholic Latinos had remained stable at 70.2 percent (or almost 25 million) in 2002. This apparent stability, however, is largely due to the significant influx of Catholics into the United States from Latin America and especially from Mexico, a country that has one of the highest rates of Catholicism in Latin America. The US Census, for example, reported that the Latino population increased by 58 percent between 1990 and 2000. The relatively high overall percentage of Catholics is also due to the creative work of a growing number of liberationist and activist Latino priests, Catholic youth programs, social programs that address the needs of the poor and immigrants, increased lay participation, and the growth of Charisma Missions and other Catholic Charismatic movements." "Hispanic Churches in American Public Life: Summary of Findings" by Gastón Espinosa, Virgilio Elizondo, and Jesse Miranda published in *Interim Reports,* Center for the Study of Latino Religion, University of Notre Dame (January 2003), 14. Espinosa was the research director of the project, an ecumenically sponsored three-year survey of almost three thousand Hispanics nationwide to determine the influence of religion on their personal and public lives. The HCAPL research project, as it came to be called, was funded by The Pew Charitable Trusts. Another recent study, headed by Anthony M. Stevens-Arroyo of the Program for the Analysis of Religion Among Latinos/as (PARAL) and that draws from the American Religious Identification Survey (ARIS 2000), is entitled "Religious Identification Among Hispanics in the

United States, 2001." Stevens-Arroyo concludes that, by and large, "Hispanics are not leaving Catholicism for the Pentecostal or Protestant churches. The Protestant share of the Hispanic adult population held steady (26 percent in 1990 and 25 percent in 2001), while Pentecostals increased only fractionally, from a little more than 3 percent to a little less than 4 percent. But even though Catholic Latinos and Latinas did not defect to other denominations, ARIS/PARAL reports that the Catholic share of the nation's Hispanic population has dropped from 66 percent in 1990 to 57 percent." Stevens-Arroyo writing in *America,* July 7, 2003, "Correction, Sí; Defection, No." Stevens-Arroyo proceeds to respond to the obvious resulting question: "If the Catholic Hispanics from 1990 did not go to the Protestant churches, where did they go? The ARIS/PARAL report shows that the fastest growing religious group among Hispanics was of those adults who profess 'no religion.' Their percentages rose from 6 percent in 1990 to 13 percent in 2001." In an explanation for this apparent drop in religious practice, Stevens-Arroyo explains, "It appears...that raising the standards for Catholic membership since 1985 has helped reverse a previous trend for Hispanic Catholics to join Protestant churches. That policy, however, may have created a new 'problem' for Hispanics who have defined their religious identity by cultural Catholicism. Instead of thinking of them as having 'defected,' it is probably better to consider these Hispanics as 'corrected' by a change in church policy. Correction rather than defection may also be a cause for pastoral optimism. When taking into account the relative youth of this group and the diaspora to new areas, there may be a temporary quality to the condition of 'no religion' for Hispanics. In any case, it would appear that the increasing diversity among U.S. Hispanics calls for more variation in approaches to evangelization and pastoral care."

64. J. L. González, *Mañana: Christian Theology from a Hispanic Perspective* (Nashville: Abingdon Press, 1990), 71–72.

65. A. F. Deck, "Fundamentalism and the Hispanic Catholic," *America,* January 26, 1985, 64–66.

66. On a more positive note, the U.S. Catholic Church has taken a strong advocacy role at various times in history. Among

these champions is the man who was archbishop of San Antonio from 1941 to 1969. See Stephen A. Privett, SJ, *The U.S. Catholic Church and Its Hispanic Members: The Pastoral Vision of Archbishop Robert E. Lucey* (San Antonio: Trinity University Press, 1988).

67. Rodríguez, "Realitics for Hispanics," 9. See also his article, "The Hispanic Community and Church Movements: Schools of Leadership," in *Hispanic Catholic Culture in the U.S.: Issues and Concerns,* ed. J. P. Dolan and A. F. Figueroa Deck, SJ (Notre Dame, IN: University of Notre Dame Press, 1994), 206–39.

68. See *Prophetic Vision: Pastoral Reflections on the National Plan for Hispanic Ministry,* ed. Soledad Galeron, Rosa María Icaza, and Rosendo Urrabazo (Kansas City: Sheed & Ward in cooperation with the staff of The Mexican American Cultural Center in San Antonio, Texas, 1992). The work is a collection of essays written by leading pastoral theologians.

69. For a description of the *encuentros* and a characterization of their spirit, see González, *Mañana,* 65. For an appreciation of their overall contribution, see Kenneth G. Davis, "Encuentros, National Pastoral," in *New Catholic Encyclopedia,* vol. 19 (Washington, DC: The Catholic University of America, Supplement 1989–95), 117–19. The most recent one, entitled "The National Celebration of Jubilee 2000, Encuentro 2000: Many Faces in God's House," was held in Los Angeles, California, from July 6 to 9, 2000. Unlike the others, whose focus was more within the U.S. Hispanic Church, this one was hosted by the Hispanic community as a way of working toward greater unity among the different groups that make up the Church. As a result of Encuentro 2000, in 2002 the U.S. bishops published an addendum to the 1987 pastoral plan. This addendum is entitled "Encuentro and Mission: A Renewed Pastoral Framework for Hispanic Ministry." This document, which builds upon and extends the 1987 plan, can be found at http://www.usccb.org/hispanicaffairs/encuentromission.shtml.

70. USCC, "National Pastoral Plan for Hispanic Ministry" *Origins* 26 (December 10, 1987): 5.

71. K. G. Davis, "Father, We're Not in Kansas Anymore," *The Priest,* July 1990, 16.

72. A. F. Deck, "As I See It," *Company* 6 (Fall 1988): 28.

73. Rosa María Icaza, "Spirituality of the Mexican American People," *Worship* 63 (May 1989): 232. For a brief, historical overview of the transformative power of popular religion in the Southwest, see Alberto L. Pulido, "Mexican American Catholicism in the Southwest: The Transformation of a Popular Religion," in *Perspectives in Mexican American Studies,* vol. 4 (Tucson: Mexican American Studies and Research Center, University of Arizona, Tucson, 1993), 93–108.

74. Ibid.

75. *The Hispanic Presence: Challenge and Commitment* (Washington, DC: U.S. Catholic Conference of Bishops, 1984), # 6.

76. See V. P. Elizondo, *The Future Is Mestizo: Life Where Cultures Meet* (New York: Meyer-Stone, 1988); A. F. Deck, *The Second Wave: Hispanic Ministry and the Evangelization of Cultures* (New York: Paulist Press, 1989); M. P. Aquino, *Our Cry for Life: Feminist Theology from Latin America* (New York: Orbis Books, 1993).

77. USCC, *The Hispanic Presence,* # 11.

78. See J. P. Fitzpatrick, SJ, "The Hispanic Poor in the American Catholic Middle-Class Church," *Thought* 63 (June 1988): 189–200.

Chapter 3

1. See Sandra M. Schneiders, IHM, "Religion and Spirituality: Strangers, Rivals, or Partners?" (public lecture, Santa Clara University, February 6, 2000).

2. See my entry "Hispanic Spirituality," in *The New Westminster Dictionary of Christian Spirituality,* ed. Philip Sheldrake (Louisville: Westminster John Knox Press, 2005), 338–41. Much of this section is an expansion of some of those ideas, especially as they relate to Mexico.

3. See Ellen McCracken, *New Latina Narrative: The Feminine Space of Postmodern Ethnicity* (Tucson: University of Arizona Press, 1999).

4. From a personal e-mail (in Spanish) sent to the author, dated November 3, 2003. The translation is mine.

5. See "Ignored Virgin or Unaware Women: A Mexican-American Protestant Reflection on the Virgin of Guadalupe" by Nora O. Lozano-Díaz, in *A Reader in Latina Feminist Theology: Religion and Justice*, ed. María Pilar Aquino, Daisy L. Machado, and Jeanette Rodríguez (Austin: University of Texas Press, 2002), 204–16.

6. Mexican Council for the Development of Indigenous People (CDI). Only 6 percent of the population, however, speaks an indigenous language. http://en.wikipedia.org/wiki/Languages_of_Mexico, accessed on June 29, 2006.

7. While historically Mexico's religious diversity paled in comparison to the geographic, economic, and cultural manifestations evident even to this day, the fact remains that Mexico's religiosity was not and is not uniform today, as the increasing number of Mexican Protestants, Jehovah's Witnesses, and Mormons attest.

8. Allan Figueroa Deck, SJ, "La Raza Cósmica: Rediscovering the Hispanic Soul," *The Critic* 37, no. 3 (Spring 1993): 46–53. Much of this section is indebted to his insights.

9. Deck, "La Raza Cósmica," 48.

10. Deck, "La Raza Cósmica," 49.

11. After spending a Good Friday at the live way of the cross, Cuban-American theologian Roberto Goizueta decided to entitle his book on Hispanic theology after a hymn that was sung there, "Caminemos con Jesús" (Let us walk with Jesus). See *Caminemos Con Jesús: Toward a Hispanic/Latino Theology of Accompaniment* (Maryknoll, NY: Orbis Books, 1995).

12. The phrase, which can be translated as "Mass, Table, and Muse," is also the title of an excellent collection of pastoral articles. See *Misa, Mesa y Musa: Liturgy in the U.S. Hispanic Church*, comp. and ed. Kenneth G. Davis, OFM, conv. (Schiller Park, IL: World Library Publications, 1997).

13. Octavio Paz, *The Labyrinth of Solitude: Life and Thought in Mexico,* trans. Lysander Kemp (New York: Grove Press, 1961), 50. Although the original essays were penned more than fifty years ago, this book has retained a unique position in the interpretation of Mexican thought for the modern world.

14. See Roberto S. Goizueta, "Fiesta: Life in the Subjunctive," in *From the Heart of Our People: Latino/a Explorations in Catholic Systematic Theology,* ed. Orlando O. Espín and Miguel H. Díaz (Maryknoll, NY: Orbis Books, 1999), 84–99.

15. I am indebted to Fernando Alvarez Lara, SJ, for these observations from an October 1, 2003 interview. Born in the United States of America and a resident of Camargo, Chihuahua, until the age of fifteen, he came back to the States to study.

16. In terms of not only what Hispanics bring to liturgy but also how they are challenged by it, see Francis Buckley, "Popular Religiosity and Sacramentality: Learning from Hispanics a Deeper Sense of Symbol, Ritual, and Sacrament," *The Living Light* 27, no. 4 (Summer 1991): 351–60.

17. I do not mean to imply that all Mexican fiestas are either religious (for example, the *fiestas patrias* that celebrate Mexican Independence from Spain) or are, for that matter, celebrated in this visionary spirit. As with other cultures, there may often be excesses that need to be challenged pastorally. A case that comes to mind is the sometimes unsupervised, easy availability of liquor at a fiesta, which can be very problematic, especially for young people. Two resources for understanding the fiesta as related to the sacraments are *Primero Dios: Hispanic Liturgical Resource* (Chicago: LTP, 1997) by Mark R. Francis and Arturo Pérez-Rodríguez and *La Vida Sacra: A Contemporary Hispanic Sacramental Theology* (Lanham, MD: Rowman & Littlefield, 2006) by James Empereur and Eduardo Fernández.

18. Quoted in "Hispanic Gang Members Keep Strong Family Ties," by Seth Mydans in the *New York Times,* September 11, 1995.

19. See chapter 7 of Empereur and Fernández, *La Vida Sacra.*

20. Dean H. Hoge, William D. Dinges, Mary Johnson, SND de N, and Juan González, Jr., *Young Adult Catholics: Religion in the*

Culture of Choice (Notre Dame, IN: University of Notre Dame Press, 2001), 119.

21. See Virgilio Elizondo's *Guadalupe: Mother of the New Creation* (Maryknoll, NY: Orbis Books, 1997).

22. For greater elaboration on this general way in which Hispanics make moral decisions, see Samuel García, *Dignidad: Ethics Through Hispanic Eyes* (Nashville: Abingdon Press, 1997).

23. Frederick John Dalton, *The Moral Vision of Cesar Chávez* (Maryknoll, NY: Orbis Books, 2003). For a discussion of how Latino popular religion continues to be both a symbolic resource of meaning and a potential agent for change in concrete social and political areas, see Allan F. Deck and Christopher Tirres, "Latino Popular Religion and the Struggle for Justice," in *Religion, Race and Justice in a Changing America,* ed. Gary Orfield and Holly Lebowitz Rossi (New York: Century Foundation, 1999), 139–210.

24. María Pilar Aquino, "Perspectives on a Latina's Feminist Liberation Theology," in *Frontiers of Hispanic Theology in the United States,* ed. Allan Figueroa Deck (Maryknoll, NY: Orbis Books, 1992), 23–40. This quote is on p. 36.

25. Orlando Espín, "Tradition and Popular Religion: An Understanding of the *Sensus Fidelium,*" in *Frontiers of Hispanic Theology in the United States,* ed. Allan Figueroa Deck (Maryknoll, NY: Orbis Books, 1992), 62–87. This quote is on p. 71.

26. For an example of the pedagogical aspects of popular religion, see Anita de Luna, MCDP, *Faith Formation and Popular Religion: Lessons from the Tejano Experience* (Lanham, MD: Rowman & Littlefield, 2002).

Chapter 4

1. Sylvia Chacón, ASC, "The Aesthetics of Reconciliation: Embracing Ritual and Art" (unpublished master's of theological studies' synthesis paper, Jesuit School of Theology at Berkeley, December 2003), 22, note 73.

2. Much of this discussion is based on *Faith Expressions of Hispanics in the Southwest,* 3rd ed. (rev.), rev. and ed. Sister Rosa María Icaza, CCVI (San Antonio, TX: Mexican American Cultural

Center, 2003). It is the fruit of a series of working sessions held in San Antonio, Albuquerque, and Los Angeles during the summer of 1977, facilitated by Reverend Luis Maldonado of the Pontifical University of Salamanca, an international expert on popular piety who collaborated on the project with Reverend Juan Romero and Reverend Juan Alfaro, OSB. According to the published report, the purpose of the workshop was "to reach a deeper understanding of the dimensions of popular piety and the underlying attitudes of the people, especially Mexican Americans in the Southwest, in order to discover criteria for the appreciation of its values. Another purpose was to create a vehicle for sharing insights into the soul of a people with pastors, bishops, religious superiors, and those responsible for the formation of future ministers for the Spanish-speaking in the U.S. It is a long-range purpose of this project to accelerate the process of study of the practices of popular piety in other regions, through similar workshops, so that they may more consciously and explicitly enrich liturgical celebrations of the Spanish-speaking and of the whole American church" (1–2). For further background on popular religiosity, see Luis Maldonado's *Introducción a la Religiosidad Popular* (Santander: Sal Terrae, 1985).

3. As quoted in "Our Lady of Guadalupe: Let Me Share a Journey with You" by Eduardo C. Fernández, SJ, in *The Rio Grande Catholic* 6, no. 6 (December 1996). The bulk of the article is presented in this chapter.

4. In the novel *The Years With Laura Díaz* by Carlos Fuentes, the character José Maura makes the following statement about the Virgin of Guadalupe: "She's a Christian and an Indian Virgin, but she's also the Virgin of Israel, the Jewish mother of the long-awaited Messiah. On top of that, she has an Arabic name, Guadalupe, river of wolves. How many cultures for the price of a single image!" As quoted in "Years of the Dead: The Elusive, Chaotic Mexico" by David Garza, *The Austin Chronicle*, October 27, 2000, 62.

5. Ibid. These words are taken from the *Nican Mopua*, one of the oldest known accounts of the apparitions. See Elizondo's *Guadalupe: Mother of the New Creation* (Maryknoll, NY: Orbis Books, 1977). Recent years, especially since the canonization of Juan

Diego, have seen many publications questioning the historicity of the apparitions. Several of the works merit serious attention, especially those that are sensitive to the times in which the devotion became popular. My purpose here is not to refute those claims, but simply, in imitating Father Elizondo, to demonstrate the living faith around this devotion whose credibility among the people is not based solely on written texts. For a study of her importance for Mexican-American women, see Jeanette Rodríguez, *Our Lady of Guadalupe: Faith and Empowerment Among Mexican-American Women* (Austin: University of Texas Press, 1994). Other recent important historical works include David A. Brading, *Mexican Phoenix: Our Lady of Guadalupe: Image and Tradition Across Five Centuries* (Cambridge: Cambridge University Press, 2001); Stafford Poole, *Our Lady of Guadalupe: The Origins and Sources of a Mexican National Symbol, 1531–1797* (Tucson: University of Arizona Press, 1995); and most recently, Timothy Matovina, *Guadalupe and Her Faithful: Latino Catholics in San Antonio, from Colonial Origins to the Present* (Baltimore: Johns Hopkins University Press, 2005). From a Protestant perspective, see Maxwell E. Johnson, *The Virgin of Guadalupe: Theological Reflections of an Anglo-Lutheran Liturgist* (Lanham, MD: Rowman & Littlefield, 2002). For a collection of contemporary essays, see *The Treasure of Guadalupe*, ed. Virgilio Elizondo, Allan Figueroa Deck, and Timothy Matovina (Lanham, MD: Rowman & Littlefield, 2006).

6. For a script of these in both Spanish and an English translation, together with those of other traditional works, see Larry Torres, trans., *Six Nuevomexicano Folk Dramas for Advent Season* (Albuquerque: University of New Mexico Press, 1999).

7. For a detailed description of these celebrations, together with pastoral insights and suggested prayers, see Miguel Arias, Arturo Pérez-Rodríguez, and Mark Francis, *La Navidad Hispana: At Home and at Church* (Chicago: Liturgy Training Publications, 2000). In regards to the religious meaning behind the piñata, for example, they note: "The novenas for the feast of Guadalupe and the *posadas* usually end with piñatas and refreshments. The Franciscan missionaries originally used piñatas as catechetical tools, teaching that their customary seven projections with sticks represented the faithful

person's continuous struggle with Satan in order to regain the grace that Satan had taken away. When the piñata was broken, 'grace'—candy, fruit and favors—poured down" (19).

8. *Faith Expressions,* 14. For a moving description of Ash Wednesday in the town of San José de Gracia, Jalisco, in Mexico, one that accents the role of family, community, the home, food, pilgrimage, and the self-acknowledgment as a Christian, see Miguel Arias Gutierrez, "En La Casa, En La Iglesia," *Liturgy* 15, no. 1 (Fall 1998): 31–34.

9. For a thoughtful reflection on the Vía Crucis and Mexican-American popular religious traditions, particularly as experienced in the Pilsen neighborhood of Chicago, see Roberto S. Goizueta's essay, "The Symbolic World of Mexican American Religion," in *Horizons of the Sacred: Mexican Traditions in U.S. Catholicism,* ed. Timothy Matovina and Gary Riebe-Estrella, SVD (Ithaca and London: Cornell University Press, 2002). Describing the transformative power of popular religion as it enters public space, Goizueta reports the observation of a young man named Jorge who has played various roles in the Good Friday procession. "Jorge notes that the number of bars that formally dotted the 18th Street route of the Via Crucis has dwindled over the years as people have brought their prayers into the street, praying for and to the alcoholics themselves. For Jorge, the social power of the sacred is clearly palpable; the signs of that power are visible on the street itself" (129).

10. *Faith Expressions,* 15.

11. In my opinion, the best video presentation to date, which describes these events, especially from the perspective of people, is Adán Medrano's 28-minute work entitled *Soul of the City/Alma del Pueblo* (Houston: JM Communications, 1996). I also recommend Thomas Kane's 49-minute video, *Fiesta! Celebrations at San Fernando* (Mahwah, NJ: Paulist Press, 1999) and Gayla Jamison and J. R. Gutierrez's *La Gran Posada: A Christmas Celebration* (San Antonio: Hispanic Telecommunications Network and Family Theater Productions, 1998). It runs 57 minutes. For a focus on the relevance of the Posadas, especially in the case of three undocu-

mented teenagers in the Los Angeles area, see *Posada: A Night to Cross all Borders* (Los Angeles: 2007). The DVD runs 57 minutes.

12. For moving stories that were recorded in de Porres's cause for beatification, as well as a discussion of the theology behind them, see Alejandro García-Rivera's *St. Martin de Porres: The "Little Stories" and the Semiotics of Culture* (Maryknoll, NY: Orbis Books, 1995).

13. See "A Saint Who Guides Migrants to a Promised Land" by Ginger Thompson, *New York Times,* August 14, 2002.

14. See "Los Milagros de Juan Soldado" by Sam Quiñones in *Día Siete* 157 (Suplemento de *El Despertador S.A. de C.V.* [México, D.F.]), 37–43. Translation of quote is my own.

15. To some, these customs may seem quite odd. Father Greg Bauman, a Jesuit priest who has worked in a poor section of Los Angeles for years, had this to say about these events: "In Anglo culture an altar for the dead seems bizarre, because we divorce ourselves from the fact that we die...we try to put it off in the corner and only face it when we have to. The Latino culture is not afraid of death...when you age you don't have to be ashamed." Quoted in "Días de los Muertos: Public Ritual, Community Renewal, and Popular Religion in Los Angeles" by Lara Medina and Gilbert R. Cadena, in *Horizons of the Sacred,* 87.

16. Alejandro García-Rivera, "Día de los Muertos: Fiesta Familiar. Day of the Dead: A Family Reunion," in *Momento Católico* (Chicago: Claretian Publications, 1992). For a way of integrating the celebration into the liturgy, see also Raúl Gómez, "The Day of the Dead: Celebrating the Continuity of Life and Death," *Liturgy* 14, no. 1 (Spring 1997): 28–40, as well as chapter 7 of Empereur and Fernández's *La Vida Sacra.*

17. As reported in Medina and Cadena, "Dias de los Muertos," 93.

18. This need for listening on the part of pastoral agents was mentioned again and again by persons I interviewed in the writing of this book.

19. See Gerald F. Muller, CSC, *With Life and Laughter: The Life of Father Pro* (Boston: Pauline Books and Media, 1996).

20. When I was growing up in El Paso, Texas, on the U.S.-Mexican border, for example, our pastor was able to renew the tradition of the *posadas* by procuring such materials as texts, music, candy, and piñatas from nearby Ciudad Juárez, Mexico. Although born in the United States of America, he worked for a time in Mexico and his parents had been immigrants, and so he was better able to understand the importance of this celebration for welcoming newcomers to the parish neighborhoods and for forming community.

21. The authors explain their context and the use of the plural, which is not normally the case: "We use the plural form, *Días,* to emphasize the numerous days of preparation, as well as the several days that the participants actually spend honoring and communing with their dead. As a third-generation Chicana and Chicano, we have shared in the expansion of these celebrations in Los Angeles and San Francisco for the last twenty years. The order of the ritual components may vary from place to place, but the components themselves remain essentially the same. Our work at several universities in Southern California introduced the tradition to several campus communities in the early 1990s. The exuberant response affirms that the tradition reflects both the rich spirituality and the political sensibilities of Chicanas/os" (72).

22. *Faith Expressions,* 22.

23. To date, the best comprehensive book on the pastoral celebration and integration of these rites into the Church's official liturgy is the excellent work by Arturo Pérez-Rodríguez and Mark Francis entitled *Primero Dios: Hispanic Liturgical Resource* (Chicago: Liturgy Training Publications, 1997). Its descriptions, pastoral notes, and suggested liturgies are a welcome resource for doing ministry among Latinos in the United States of America. James Empereur and I drew heavily from it for our work, *La Vida Sacra: A Contemporary Hispanic Sacramental Theology.* In this book, we discuss how each of the seven sacraments is celebrated in the Latino community together with what Latinos bring to the larger Church's sacramental tradition. In addition, for each of the sacraments, we list several challenges to Latinos posed by the evangelical values the sacraments celebrate.

24. For an excellent treatment of this history, written by one who played a key role in its development, see Arturo J. Pérez, "The History of Hispanic Liturgy since 1965," in *Hispanic Catholic Culture in the U.S.: Issues and Concerns,* ed. Jay P. Dolan and Allan Figueroa Deck (Notre Dame, IN: University of Notre Dame Press, 1994), 360–408.

25. Pérez-Rodríguez and Francis, *Primero Dios.*

26. See *Primero Dios.*

27. *Faith Expressions,* 24. For an explanation of the origins of these type of marriage customs, current use, and relevance to the official marriage liturgy, see the bilingual booklet prepared by Reverend Raúl Gómez, SDS, Reverend Heliodoro Lucatero, and Ms. Sylvia Sánchez, entitled *Gift and Promise: Customs and Traditions in Hispanic Rites of Marriage,* 2nd ed. (Portland, OR: Instituto Hispano de Litúrgia/Oregon Catholic Press, 2005).

28. For an extensive treatment of these and other rites of passage, see *Primero Dios* and *La Vida Sacra.*

29. See *Quinceañera: Celebration of Life, Guidebook for the Presider of the Religious Rite/Quinceañera, Celebración de la Vida, Guía Para Los Que Presiden el Rito Religioso* (San Antonio: Mexican American Cultural Center, 1999). In the introductory notes the writers mention some of the priests and other pastoral agents' misgivings concerning the celebration as it is commonly held today: "It [the religious rite] may be as complicated as a modern day wedding with limousines, caterers, paid musicians, fancy clothes or costumes, elaborate flower and arch decorations, and more than one priest presiding. For many priests the excesses of some families in the elaborate 'extras' and the apparent lack of religious significance for many teenagers, result in outright rejection of all such ceremonies as mere social events. Even those sympathetic to the popular religion of Latinos find it difficult to participate in a set of symbols that seem to have only superficial meaning. It does not have to be that way...As more pastoral agents are taught the rich significance of this custom then the preparation for the ritual takes on more of an evangelizing and catechetical activity" (xii).

30. See chapter 7 of *La Vida Sacra*. For an excellent resource for helping the minister to bridge the cultural gap in the area of ministering to the sick, especially in light of *curanderismo* (defined by Rafaela G. Castro as "the folk process of healing, similar to much contemporary alternative medicine in its holistic approach, with no recognition of a separation between the mind and body"), see Kenneth G. Davis, "Annoying the Sick? Cultural Considerations for the Celebration of a Sacrament," *Worship* 78, no. 1 (January 2004): 35–50.

31. *Faith Expressions*, 27.

32. As an example of how the saints help to bring us together, I am reminded of my grandfather who would, on occasion, take a statue to be blessed together with someone with whom he wanted to be a *compadre*.

33. *Faith Expressions*, 34–40.

34. In "The Hispanic Shift: Continuity Rather than Conversion?" Kenneth Davis examines the appeal of Pentecostalism to Hispanics and the consequences of such a massive shift in religious affiliation. He surmises that one of the major reasons is Pentecostalism's similarities to popular Catholicism (in *Journal of Hispanic/Latino Theology* 1, no. 3 [May 1994]: 68–79). See also Allan Figueroa Deck, "The Challenge of Evangelical/Pentecostal Christianity to Hispanic Catholicism," in *Hispanic Catholic Culture in the United States*, ed. Jay P. Dolan and Allan Figueroa Deck (Notre Dame, IN: University of Notre Dame, 1994), 427–28.

35. Virgilio Elizondo tells the story of being asked by a young couple going off to war to bless their tattoos of Our Lady of Guadalupe. When he asked them why they didn't just wear a medal of her, they responded, "We might lose the medal, but the tattoos will always be with us."

36. Known as the *presentación*, this practice is further discussed in our book, *La Vida Sacra*.

37. *Faith Expressions*, 35.

38. I remember once driving by a church in Oakland, California, where, after blessed ashes had been given out all day, a small bowl filled with them was placed on a small table in front of

the locked doors, next to a lit votive candle. A family was putting the ashes on the foreheads of their children.

39. *Faith Expressions,* 38.

40. For good, practical points for drawing upon pilgrimages as ways of spiritual growth, see Virgilio Elizondo, "Pastoral Opportunities of Pilgrimages," in *Pilgrimage,* ed. Virgil Elizondo and Sean Freyne (Maryknoll, NY: Orbis Books), 107–14.

41. *Faith Expressions* explains this devotional practice, which may seem very alien to many Catholics in the United States: "Usually a *promesa* (promise) has two basic elements: the petition of a favor and the *manda* or vow which is the fulfillment of stipulations accompanying the vow. *Promesas* are specially important for people in cases of sickness when a doctor says *'que no tiene remedio'* (there is no medical cure). Once a favor or request is considered granted the *manda* takes place. It can take the form of a stipend for Masses, of lighting a candle, *veladora,* either at a church, shrine or at home, or going on one's knees, *de rodillas* up to the altar of a chosen church or shrine to leave an *ofrenda* (offering). Persons fulfilling a *manda* generally offer a *milagrito* or *exvoto* usually consisting of gold, silver or bronze 'charms,' miniature objects in the form of the human body or part of the body that has been cured. They may also offer strands of hair or a portion of one's long hair, especially in the case of women. It is also customary to leave in the shrine or church a picture of the person cured or some letter testifying to the help received" (39–40).

42. A helpful summary of Segundo Galilea's pastoral approaches to popular religion are presented in Robert J. Schreiter's well-known work, *Constructing Local Theologies* (Maryknoll, NY: Orbis Books, 1985), 141–43.

43. Allan Figueroa Deck, SJ, "A Latino Practical Theology: Mapping the Road Ahead," *Theological Studies* 65 (2004): 297. In the same article, Deck invokes such writers as Francis and Pérez-Rodríguez *(Primero Dios)* and Kenneth G. Davis, the editor of *Misa, Mesa y Musa: Liturgy in the U.S. Hispanic Church* (Schiller Park, IL: World Library Publications, 1997) to say that "these authors make the fundamental point that the starting point for the liturgical inculturation of Hispanic Catholicism must be popular

religion. Liturgical theology and familiarity with the official norms constitute an important second moment" (291, note 32). See also *The Directory on Popular Piety and the Liturgy: Principles and Guidelines: A Commentary*, ed. Peter C. Phan (Collegeville, MN: The Liturgical Press, 2005).

44. For an exploration of some of the reasons why popular piety is on the rise even outside the Latino communities, see Patrick L. Malloy, "The Re-Emergence of Popular Religion Among Non-Hispanic American Catholics," *Worship* 72, no. 1 (January 1998): 2–25.

Chapter 5

1. This chapter, especially its featured theologians, owes a good amount to chapter 2, "The History of U.S. Hispanic Theology: 1972–1998" of my book, *La Cosecha: Harvesting Contemporary United States Hispanic Theology (1972–1998)* (Collegeville, MN: The Liturgical Press, 2000), 35–93.

2. Among the earliest comprehensive articles written on the subject are Fernando Segovia, "A New Manifest Destiny: The Emerging Theological Voice of Hispanic Americans," *Religious Studies Review* 17, no. 2 (April 1991): 102–9; Arturo Bañuelas, "U.S. Hispanic Theology," *Missiology* 20, no. 2 (April 1991): 275–300; and Allan F. Deck's introduction to *Frontiers of Hispanic Theology in the United States* (New York: Orbis Books, 1992). Two recent books on the topic are Fernández, *La Cosecha*, and Miguel H. Díaz, *On Being Human: U.S. Hispanic and Rahnerian Perspectives* (Maryknoll, NY: Orbis Books, 2001).

3. Justo L. González, *Mañana: Christian Theology from a Hispanic Perspective* (Nashville: Abingdon Press, 1990), 75.

4. Justo L. González, "Contextual Theologies," in *Essential Theological Terms* (Louisville: Westminster John Knox Press, 2005), 38.

5. Ibid.

6. Ibid. Other forms that could be added to this list are Asian-American theology, Native American theology, and gay/lesbian theology. For an excellent introduction to contextual theology, see

Stephen B. Bevans, *Models of Contextual Theology,* rev. ed. (Maryknoll, NY: Orbis Books, 2002).

7. Virgil P. Elizondo, "Educación Religiosa para el Mexico-Norteamericano," *Catequesis Latinoamericana* (1972). See also his *Christianity* and *Culture,* published by Our Sunday Visitor Press in 1975.

8. V. P. Elizondo, *The Future Is Mestizo* (Boulder: University of Colorado Press, 2000), 15.

9. Ibid., 26.

10. The word *mestizo* has traditionally been used to designate a person who is a mixture of both indigenous and European blood. *Mestizaje* refers to the process. Justo González, having mentioned that Virgilio Elizondo in his writings has related, because of their marginal status, the condition of Mexican-Americans in the United States of America and of Galileans in ancient Judaism, explains the meaning of the word as used in Hispanic theology: "A *mestizo*—strictly speaking, a 'mixed breed'—is a person who stands between cultures, considered alien by both, and yet creating a new culture that may well be the vanguard for both dominant cultures. Latino and Latina theologians have developed this theme as a paradigm for understanding their situation, in which they no longer belong to the culture of their homelands, and yet they do not fully belong to the culture of the United States" ("Latino/a Theology," in *Essential Theological Terms,* 96). Elizondo's clearest articulation of this theological application is found in *Galilean Journey: The Mexican American Promise* (Maryknoll, NY: Orbis Books, 1983).

11. Elizondo, *The Future Is Mestizo,* 108ff.

12. To the extent that is possible within the limitations of this chapter, I have sought to present *un bocadito,* or a taste, of each of the writings of the major theologians.

13. Allan Figueroa Deck, "A New Vision of a Tattered Friendship," *Grito del Sol* 4, no. l (1974): 87–93; Marina Herrera, "La Teología en el Mundo de Hoy," *Páginas Banilejas* (July 1974).

14. For a description of how ACHTUS was born, see Deck's introduction to *Frontiers.* The Academy continues its work today and has over one hundred members.

15. Justo González, "Orthopraxis," in *Essential Theological Terms,* 125.

16. See Deck, *Frontiers of Hispanic Theology* (xviii–xix), for an interesting comparison between Latin America's theology of liberation and U.S. Hispanic theology.

17. Joe Holland and Peter Henriot, in *Social Analysis: Linking Faith and Justice* (Maryknoll, NY: Orbis Books, 1983), describe this method as the "pastoral circle." This method incorporates the well-known "ver, juzgar, y actuar" approach suggested at Puebla, a meeting of the Latin American bishops held in Mexico in 1979. Its strength is its emphasis on the ongoing relationship between reflection and action. Like the hermeneutic circle—a method of interpretation in which older theories are questioned in light of new situations—the pastoral circle allows for ongoing renewal of both theory and practice. These authors credit both Paulo Freire (*The Pedagogy of the Oppressed* [New York: Herder and Herder, 1970]) and Juan Luis Segundo (*The Liberation of Theology* [Maryknoll, NY: Orbis Books, 1976]) for their contributions to this model of analysis.

18. A. M. Isasi-Díaz, "'*Apuntes*' for an Hispanic Women's Theology of Liberation," *Apuntes* 6, no. 3 (Fall 1986): 61–70. It was reprinted in the collection edited by Justo L. González entitled *Voces: Voices from the Hispanic Church* (Nashville: Abingdon Press, 1992), 24–31. Elsewhere, González summarizes the meaning of *mujerista* theology: "While agreeing with much of feminist theology, mujerista theology insists that such theology has been so concerned about issues and perspectives in the dominant culture that it is unable to express the experience, the oppression, and the hopes of minority women—particularly Hispanic women. Also, while agreeing with much of Latino theology, mujerista theology points out that Latino theology is so concerned over issues of culture, class, and race that it often does not pay sufficient attention to gender issues. Hence the need for a distinguishing name: 'mujerista'—from the Spanish *mujer,* woman. The methodology of mujerista theology thus stresses the need to listen to the actual words and experiences of Latinas, and then interpreting those expressions in theological terms, rather than imposing traditional theological categories on the experienced life of

Latinas" ("Mujerista Theology," in *Essential Theological Terms,* 116–17).

19. Ada María Isasi-Díaz and Yolanda Tarango, *Hispanic Women: Prophetic Voice in the Church* (San Francisco: Harper & Row, 1988). This book is the fruit of a decade of listening and reflecting with eleven different groups.

20. A. M. Isasi-Díaz and Y. Tarango, *Hispanic Women,* ix.

21. Ada María Isasi-Díaz, *En La Lucha/In the Struggle: Elaborahng a Mujerista Theology* (Philadelphia: Fortress Press, 2003). See Jeanette Rodriguez's treatment of religious emotion as developed in the thought of William James (*Our Lady of Guadalupe: Faith and Empowerment among Mexican-American Women* [Austin: University of Texas Press, 1994], 51). For a sublime incorporation of Latinas' faith stories, see Rodriguez, *Stories We Live, Cuentos Que Vivimos: Hispanic Women's Spirituality* (New York and Mahwah, NJ: Paulist Press, 1996).

22. Clifford Geertz, *The Interpretation of Cultures* (San Francisco: Basic Books, 1973), 90.

23. See a selection of Isasi-Díaz's collected works, *Mujerista Theology: A Theology for the Twenty-First Century* (Maryknoll, NY: Orbis Books, 1996) in which she presents in the introduction a type of "road map" for understanding her work. Her treatment of such areas as liturgy, Scripture, and ethics is an example of how different perspectives shed light on each of these theological specialties. One of her latest works, in which she elaborates on how Latinas have turned marginalization into a creative space of struggle, is "*Burlando al Opresor:* Mocking/Tricking the Oppressor: Dreams and Hopes of Hispanas/Latinas and *Mujeristas,*" *Theological Studies* 65 (2004): 340–63.

24. See Holland and Henriot, *Social Analysis.*

25. Allan Figueroa Deck, *The Second Wave: Hispanic Ministry and the Evangelization of Cultures* (Mahwah, NJ: Paulist Press, 1989). Fifteen years later, he revisits this popular work in "A Latino Practical Theology: Mapping the Road Ahead," *Theological Studies* 65 (2004): 275–97.

26. (Deck, *The Second Wave* (Mahwah, NJ: Paulist Press, 1989), 1.

27. Ibid., 2.

28. Ibid.

29. See A. F. Deck, "La Raza Cósmica: Rediscovering the Hispanic Soul," *The Critic* 37, no. 3 (Spring 1993): 46–53.

30. See A. F. Deck, "A Christian Perspective on the Reality of Illegal Immigration," *Social Thought* (Fall 1978): 39–53.

31. For a history of Latino popular Catholicism in the United States, see his chapter "Popular Catholicism among Latinos," in *Hispanic Catholic Culture in the U.S.: Issues and Concerns,* ed. J. P. Dolan and A. F. Deck, SJ (Notre Dame, IN: University of Notre Dame Press, 1994), 308–59. In "A 'Multicultural' Church?: Theological Reflections from 'Below,'" in *The Multicultural Church: A New Landscape in U.S. Theologies,* ed. W. Cenkner (Mahwah, NJ: Paulist Press, 1996), 54–71, Espín expounds on the role of culture in theology. See his "Popular Religion as an Epistemology (of Suffering)," *Journal of Hispanic/Latino Theology* 2, no. 2 (November 1994): 55–78. In this article, he dialogues with other theologians and social scientists to present a hypothetical position in search of an authentic Latino epistemology. "The problem...is how [Latinos] explain their suffering, know it as suffering, and make sense (at least some sense) of it" (74). Here he argues that popular religion plays a very important role epistemologically. Finally, in "Popular Catholicism: Alienation or Hope?" in *Hispanic/Latino Theology: Challenge and Promise,* ed. F. F. Segovia and A. M. Isasi-Díaz (Minneapolis: Fortress Press, 1996), 307–24, Espín presents a critical view of popular religion, one that takes into account both its alienating and liberating potential. He is not so naive as to think that hegemonic influences have not made their way into popular religion. In 1997, Espín published a collection of six of his key articles that he entitled *The Faith of the People: Theological Reflections on Popular Catholicism* (Maryknoll, NY: Orbis Books, 1997). Both the foreword by Roberto Goizueta and the introduction by Espín provide a skillful framework for understanding his contribution as well as where his research is leading him.

32. Espín explains what he means by *sensus fidelium*: "Just as important as the written texts of tradition (or, in fact, more important), however, is the *living witness and faith* of the Christian

people...the object of the study (though expressed through cultural categories, languages, and so forth, that run the gamut of human diversity) is found at the level of *intuition*. It is this 'faith-full' intuition that makes real Christian people *sense* that something is true or not vis-á-vis the gospel, or that someone is acting in accordance with the Christian gospel or not, or that something important for Christianity is not being heard. This intuition in turn allows for and encourages a belief and a style of life and prayer that express and witness to the fundamental Christian message: God as revealed in Jesus Christ. This 'faith-full' intuition is called the *sensus fidelium* (or *sensus fidei*)." O. O. Espín, "Tradition and Popular Religion: An Understanding of the *Sensus Fidelium*," in *Frontiers*, 64.

33. Orlando O. Espín, "Grace and Humanness: A Hispanic Perspective," in *We Are A People: Initiatives in Hispanic American Theology*, ed. Roberto S. Goizueta (Minneapolis: Fortress Press, 1992), 148.

34. Ibid. See also some of his works written in collaboration with Sixto J. García: "Hispanic-American Theology," in *Proceedings of the Forty-Second Annual Convention of the Catholic Theological Society in America* (CTSA, vol. 42, 1987: 114–19); "The Sources of Hispanic Theology," in *Proceedings* (CTSA, vol. 43, 1988: 122–25); and "'Lilies of the Field': A Hispanic Theology of Providence and Human Responsibility," in *Proceedings* (CTSA, vol. 44, 1989: 70–90). Also noteworthy is "Trinitarian Monotheism and the Birth of Popular Catholicism: The Case of Sixteenth-Century Mexico," *Missiology* 20, no. 2 (April 1992): 177–204.

35. Espín, in *Frontiers*, 62.

36. Dawn Gibeau, "Hispanic Theology Aims Church at Poor," *National Catholic Reporter*, September 11, 1992.

37. Ibid.

38. Espín, in *Frontiers*, 69–70.

39. Ibid., 71.

40. See "Trinitarian Monotheism and the Birth of Popular Catholicism." For a similar Trinitarian discussion, see Sixto J. García's "A Hispanic Approach to Trinitarian Theology: The

Dynamics of Celebration, Reflection, and Praxis," in *We Are A People!: Initiatives in Hispanic American Theology,* 107–32. Two recent collections he co-edited are *From the Heart of Our People: Latino/a Explorations in Catholic Systematic Theology* (Maryknoll, NY: Orbis Books, 1999) with Miguel H. Díaz; and *Futuring Our Past: Explorations in the Theology of Tradition* (Maryknoll, NY: Orbis Books, 2006) with Gary Macy.

41. María Pilar Aquino, *Aportes para una Teología desde la Mujer* (Madrid: Biblia y Fe, 1988). Among her works are "The Challenge of Hispanic Women," *Missiology* 20, no. 2 (April 1992): 261–68; "Perspectives on a Latina's Feminist Liberation Theology," in *Frontiers,* 23–40; "Doing Theology from the Perspective of Latin American Women," in *We Are A People!: Initiatives in Hispanic American Theology,* 79–105; and "Santo Domingo Through the Eyes of Women," in *Santo Domingo and Beyond: Documents and Commentaries from the Historic Meeting of the Latin American Bishops Conference,* ed. Alfred T. Hennelly, SJ (Maryknoll, NY: Orbis Books, 1994), 212–25. See also her article, "Theological Method in U.S. Latino/a Theology: Toward an Intercultural Theology for the Third Millennium," in *From the Heart of Our People: Latino/a Explorations in Catholic Systematic Theology,* ed. Orlando O. Espín and Miguel H. Díaz (Maryknoll, NY: Orbis Books, 1999), 6–48; and *A Reader in Latina Feminist Theology: Religion and Justice,* ed. María Pilar Aquino, Daisy L. Machado, and Jeanette Rodriguez (Austin: University of Texas Press, 2002).

42. Aquino, *Nuestro Clamor por la Vida: Teología Latinoamericana desde la Perspectiva de la Mujer* (San José, Costa Rica: Editorial DEI, 1992).

43. Aquino, *Our Cry for Life: Feminist Theology from Latin America* (Maryknoll, NY: Orbis Books, 1993).

44. Note her strong reliance on Latin American authors. One quickly gets the impression, given the sources she cites in numerous places, that she is a great believer in *teología de conjunto.* Arturo Bañuelas explains the term, linking it with *pastoral de conjunto* in the following manner: "U.S. Hispanic theologies are the result of a process called *pastoral de conjunto.* This process implies a method

that stresses direct involvement and analysis of reality as necessary first steps to the author's option to theologize from within the Hispanic social and pastoral context. *Pastoral de conjunto* assures that Hispanic theologizing is grounded in human experience, especially the experience of oppression. U.S. Hispanic Theology attempts to give a voice to the voiceless. As members of the community, in the *pastoral de conjunto* process theologians also see themselves as *mestizos,* articulating their own theology. This process calls for a new kind of theologian with a new type of consciousness and commitment, so that theology will not emanate from ivory-tower abstract positions, but from engagement with other Hispanos articulating their struggles and hopes for liberation. Immersed in the Hispanic reality of oppression, these theologians understand how their cultural bias influences their theological presuppositions. They admit the non-neutrality of their theology since their common project, their *teología de conjunto,* is the liberation of Hispanics as part of God's salvific plan for a new humanity." See Arturo Bañuelas, "U.S. Hispanic Theology," *Missiology* 20, no. 2 (1992): 292.

45. Aquino, "Doing Theology from the Perspective of Latin American Women," 79–105.

46. R. S. Goizueta, ed., *We Are A People!: Initiatives in Hispanic American Theology* (Philadelphia: Fortress Press, 1992), xv.

47. A key part of this lived experience is *lo cotidiano* (the emphasis on daily life), an understanding that has been one of critical feminism's most important contributions. Aquino explains its origin: "This category emerged within the context of the feminist philosophies and sociologies developed in Eastern Europe and Latin America, in the 1960s and 1970s, in order to confront ideological totalitarianism and monolithic metadiscourses current at the time. Their aim was the reinvention of the ethical and political foundations of true democracy in social life." Aquino, "Theological Method in U.S. Latino/a Theology," 38.

48. An important consideration given what has been said about the hermeneutical privilege of the poor. That is, these women, the poorest among the poor, bring an important lens to our reading of the gospel.

49. As quoted in "Doing Theology from the Perspective of Latin American Women," 96.

50. Aquino, "Perspectives on a Latina's Feminist Liberation Theology," 24.

51. Aquino, in *Frontiers*, 36.

52. Aquino, "Doing Theology from the Perspective of Latin American Women," 84, note 6.

53. Aquino, "Perspectives on a Latina's Feminist Liberation Theology," 39, note 12.

54. In his work depicting the struggles and spirituality of those who risk life and limb by illegally crossing the U.S. border from Mexico, Daniel G. Groody conveys the great meaning that the suffering Christ has for them: "These immigrants are willing to descend into the depths of hell in the desert for the people they love so that they may have better lives. Within their particular stories of hunger, thirst, estrangement, nakedness, sickness, and imprisonment we can begin to see the face of a crucified Christ (Matthew 25:31–26:2). In their suffering, the immigrants reveal the hidden mystery of Christ today." See Daniel G. Groody, *Border of Death, Valley of Life: An Immigrant Journey of Heart and Spirit* (Lanham, MD: Rowman and Littlefield Publishers, Inc., 2002), 32–33.

55. Maryknoll, NY: Orbis Books, 1995.

56. Ibid., 67, note 33 refers to such Latin American thinkers as José Vasconcelos.

57. R. S. Goizueta, "Nosotros: Toward a U.S. Hispanic Anthropology," in *Listening: Journal of Religion and Culture* 27 (winter 1992): 67.

58. Miguel H. Díaz's book, *On Being Human,* deals with the major contributions of U.S. Hispanics to theological anthropology.

59. Ibid., 56.

60. Arturo Bañuelas, "U.S. Hispanic Theology," *Missiology* 20, no. 2 (1992): 290. One of Goizueta's most recent articles, in which he argues that Latino/a popular Catholicism in the United States provides a way of recovering some of what was lost or obscured in our current more modern, rationalistic forms of Catholicism, is "The Symbolic Realism of U.S. Latino/a Popular Catholicism,"

Theological Studies 65 (2004): 255–74. Other Hispanic theologians who also stress the role of the beautiful, and for the purposes of the present analysis, as it is found in Mexican religiosity, are Alejandro García-Rivera, *The Community of the Beautiful: A Theological Aesthetics* (Collegeville, MN: A Michael Glazier Book, The Liturgical Press, 1999); Michele A. González, *Sor Juana: Beauty and Justice in the Americas* (Maryknoll, NY: Orbis Books, 2003), a view of the seventeenth-century Mexican literary figure Sor Juana Inés de la Cruz as a theologian very much ahead of her time; Ana María Pineda, RSM, "Imagenes de Dios en el Camino: Retablos, Ex-votos, Milagritos, and Murals," *Theological Studies* 65 (2004): 364–79.

61. For an insightful discussion of this mutual relationship between Protestant and Catholic Hispanics, see the foreword by Virgil P. Elizondo in Justo L. González's work *Mañana*, 9–20.

62. See *Latino Religions and Civic Activism in the United States*, ed. Gastón Espinosa, Virgilio Elizondo, and Jesse Miranda (New York: Oxford University Press, 2005).

63. Kenneth Davis, OFM, conv., "Guest Editorial," *Theological Studies* 65 (2004): 249.

Chapter 6

1. For a discussion of evangelization, especially as articulated in Paul VI's *Evangelii Nuntiandi*, and John Paul II's "new evangelization" as it relates to U.S. *Hispanic ministry*, see A. F. Deck's *The Second Wave: Hispanic Ministry and the Evangelization of Cultures* (Mahwah, NJ: Paulist Press, 1989), and his subsequent update: "A Latino Practical Theology: Mapping the Road Ahead," Theological Studies 65 (2004).

2. *Encuentro & Mission*, #20.

3. Washington, DC: U.S. Conference of Catholic Bishops (USCCB), 2002. Taking into account new demographic data from the 2000 U.S. Census, this document builds on the 1987 *National Pastoral Plan for Hispanic Ministry* in light of John Paul II's "new evangelization," his 1983 address to the assembly of CELAM (the Latin American Conference of Bishops), and his *Ecclesia in*

America (1999), together with the results of Encuentro 2000, which was held in Los Angeles, California, and attended by more than five thousand Church leaders representing 150 dioceses and 157 different ethnic groups and nationalities.

4. As cited in Deck's "A Latino Practical Theology," 278, note 8, from a report produced by the Committee for Applied Research on the Apostolate (CARA).

5. A helpful timeline, or "Historical Memory" for U.S. Catholic Hispanic ministry can be found in *¡En Marcha!* (Fall–Winter 2002): 22–26. This issue also contains important statistics about Hispanic ministry and national demographics based on the 2000 U.S. Census. In the area of the history of lay leadership, the *movimientos,* or movements, such as the Cursillo, Marriage Encounter, or the Charismatic Renewal, have played and continue to play a key role. See chapter 5 of Empereur and Fernández's *La Vida Sacra.*

6. The age at which a person comes to this country is very significant for her or his identity formation. I have heard it said that if you come after puberty, you are more likely to identify with the country you came from while if you come before, you will tend to identify more with U.S. culture.

7. The *New York Times* reports the alarming death rate of a person a day who perished trying to enter the United States of America illegally in the summer of 2003. As vigilance in the areas around such large cities as San Diego and El Paso are tightened by U.S. Border Patrol operations, persons wishing to cross have had to resort to remote areas, increasingly falling victim to the scorching desert heat and attackers seeking to rob them of the little money they carry. The article focuses on the fate of children smuggled across the border, whose parents can no longer go back and forth as easily ("Littlest Immigrants, Left in the Hands of Smugglers," November 3, 2003).

8. *¡En Marcha!* (Fall–Winter 2002): 15.

9. Reflecting on her experience of working on the U.S.-Mexican border, Sister Sylvia Chacón writes: "I noticed that both men and women [in Ciudad Juárez, Chihuahua] would more readily respond to requests for help and would need less direction than recent immigrants into El Paso, Texas, its sister city across the border. For

example, the church decorations for the feast of Our Lady of Guadalupe, posed no problem. Even though it was done the last minute, the decoration of the church was well done, while in El Paso, the women seemed more hesitant to decorate *como Dios manda* [as God asks] for fear of offending the priest, the Euro-Americans, or even some of the more 'prominent' Mexican-American parishioners.

"Confidence in their intuitive sense seemed to have eroded by crossing the border. They seem more reliant on the official ministers rather than on their experience or on the collective wisdom of their neighbors. Their sense of identity suffers as they see their lives in contrast to the American ideal; however, they cling to those elements that ground them: cultural symbols, music, language, customs, traditions…Gradually, as they begin to adapt to their new environment, some begin to distance themselves from those symbols that would identify them with their culture of origin in order to gain greater acceptance. The second generation begins to feel the contrast more and seems to make a choice to reject, change or accept their new cultural identity that puts them to live in-between worlds…A similar dynamic happened to the women when the men were present: they seemed to feel less confident in the presence of their husbands." Sylvia Chacón, "The Aesthetics of Reconciliation: Embracing Ritual and Art" (unpublished master's of theological studies synthesis paper, Jesuit School of Theology at Berkeley, December 2003), 16, note 56.

10. Dean Hoge and his fellow researchers refer to Gregory Rodríguez's and others' findings to show that "within ten years of arrival 76.3% of immigrants speak English with high proficiency." Dean Hoge, William Dinges, Mary Johnson, and Juan L. González, Jr., *Young Adult Catholics: Religion in the Culture of Choice* (Notre Dame, IN: University of Notre Dame, 2001), 117, as quoted in Deck, "A Latino Practical Theology, 294, note 38.

11. Francis and Pérez-Rodríguez, *Primero Dios: Hispanic Liturgical Resource,* 31.

12. The themes of relationality and community figure prominently in a book I co-authored with James Empereur entitled *La*

Vida Sacra: A Contemporary Hispanic Sacramental Theology (Lanham, MD: Rowman & Littlefield, 2006).

13. In light of recent studies of immigrant congregations in the United States of America, sociologist John Coleman asserts that "1) Immigrants generally become more rather than less religious than in their home countries…2) Successful immigrant parishes serve as more than just houses of worship, a place for liturgical prayer. They are also communal centers where job-training skills are honed, English language classes are held. These centers provide clinics, credit unions, housing leads, day care and also many communal meals and gatherings. At such centers the diaspora continues to be involved in home country issues (such as an election in Haiti) and to organize against American legal maneuvers to disenfranchise or disparage the immigrant population…3) In the United States, religion is one of the few differences which the culture acknowledges as legitimate. We want the country to be monolingual, and we may look askance at hyphenated loyalties, as in the phrase Korean-American, but we expect and honor religious differences. So, the immigrant congregation serves as a uniquely legitimizing cover for ethnic group agency." "Pastoral Strategies for Multicultural Parishes," *Origins* 31, no. 30 (January 10, 2002): 502.

14. For a concrete example from the Italian-American community, see Robert A. Orsi, *The Madonna of 115th Street: Faith and Community in Italian Harlem, 1880–1950* (New Haven: Yale University Press, 1985).

15. Roberto Suro et al. report that 54 percent of all Latinos now reside in the suburbs (as quoted in Deck, "A Latino Practical Theology," 276, note 3).

16. See *City, Temple, Stage: Eschatological Architecture and Liturgical Theatrics in New Spain* (Notre Dame, IN: University of Notre Dame Press, 2004) by Jaime Lara.

17. These last two examples, that from Las Cruces, New Mexico, and the one from La Verne, California, are cited in an article I wrote entitled "Seven Tips on the Pastoral Care of U.S. Catholics of Mexican Descent" published in *Chicago Studies* 36, no. 3 (December 1997): 255–69.

18. As reported in *Encuentro & Mission,* #65.

19. See "Acculturation and Mental Health" by John W. Berry and Uichol Kim in *Health and Cross-Cultural Psychology: Towards Applications,* ed. P. R. Dasen, J. W. Berry, and N. Sartorius (Newbury Park, CA: SAGE Publications, 1988), 207–36; "Counseling Hispanic Americans," chapter 14 of *Counseling the Culturally Different: Theory and Practice,* 3rd ed., by Derald Wing Sue and David Sue (New York: John Wiley & Sons, 1999), 286–303; and "The Relationship Between Acculturation and Ethnic Minority Mental Health" by Pamela Balls Organista, Kurt C. Oganista, and Karen Kurasaki in *Acculturation: Advances in Theory, Measurement, and Applied Research,* ed. Kevin M. Chun, Pamela Balls Organista, and Gerardo Marín (Washington, DC: American Psychological Association, 2003), 139–61.

20. Berry and Kim, "Acculturation and Mental Health," 211.

21. Ibid, 212.

22. Ibid.

23. Ibid.

24. Balls Organista, Organista, and Kurasaki, "Relationship," 150, refer to the work of Roger et al. (1991).

25. *Hispanic Ministry at the Turn of the New Millennium,* report of the Catholic Bishops' Committee on Hispanic Affairs (Washington, DC: National Conference of Catholic Bishops, November 1999).

26. See especially Publication 1 of *Perspectives on Hispanic Youth and Young Adult Ministry,* entitled "Welcoming the Hispanic Youth/Jóvenes in Catholic Parishes and Dioceses" by Ken Johnson-Mondragón (Stockton, CA: Instituto Fe y Vida Research and Resource Center, 2003) and, in the same series, Publication 2, his "Youth Ministry and the Socioreligious Lives of Hispanic and White Catholic Teens in the U.S., Based on the National Study of Youth and Religion (NSYR)" (Stockton, CA: Instituto Fe y Vida Research and Resource Center, 2005). Other recent, helpful articles include Gary Riebe-Estrella, SVD, "A Youthful Community: Theological and Ministerial Challenges," *Theological Studies* 65 (2004): 298–316; George Boran, CSSP, "Hispanic Catholic Youth in the United States," in *Bridging Boundaries: The Pastoral Care of U.S. Hispanics,* ed. Kenneth G. Davis and Yolanda Tarango

(Scranton: University of Scranton Press, 2000), 95–105; Arthur David Canales, "A Reality Check: Addressing Catholic Hispanic Youth Ministry in the United States of America (Part 1)," *Apuntes* 25, no. 1 (Spring 2005): 4–23, and "Reaping What We Sow: Addressing Catholic Hispanic Youth Ministry in the United States of America (Part 2)," *Apuntes* 25, no. 2 (Summer 2005): 44–74; and James Empereur and Eduardo Fernández, chapter 3, "The Passage Into Adulthood in Church and Family," in *La Vida Sacra: Contemporary Hispanic Sacramental Theology* (Lanham, MD: Rowman & Littlefield, 2006), 100–142.

27. "Cultural Values of Hispanics," put out by Hispanic Ministry in the Carolinas at www.hispanic-ministry.org/resources/brochure_values.pdf, accessed August 17, 2006.

28. Ibid.

29. *Encuentro & Mission,* #75.

30. It is no wonder, then, that as a result, only 4 percent of all lay ecclesial ministers in 1997 were Hispanic, while only 5 percent of all priests in the United States of America are Hispanic. See Ken Johnson-Mondragón, "The Educational Attainment of Hispanic Catholics in the U.S. and Its Impact on Pastoral Leadership in the Catholic Church" *¡En Marcha!* (Winter–Spring 2003): 13. *Encuentro & Mission* reports: "Priestly vocations among Hispanics are on the rise. Thirteen percent of all U.S. seminarians are Hispanic. This growth is overshadowed, however, by the ever-growing number of Hispanic Catholics, estimated to be at least 25 million—constituting nearly 40 percent of all Catholics in the United States...there is one Hispanic priest for 9,925 Hispanic Catholics in the United States. In contrast, there is one Catholic priest for every 1,230 Catholics in the general Catholic population" (#67).

31. See Dean R. Hoge and Aniedi Okure, OP, *International Priests in America: Challenges and Opportunities* (Collegeville, MN: The Liturgical Press, 2006), 30.

32. Ibid. Hoge and Okure's study, which includes many interviews from different perspectives, is groundbreaking and revelatory. I highly recommend it, especially given the fact that 16

percent of the priests serving in the United States of America since 1985 are foreign-born and the number is on the increase.

33. Alejandro Aguilera-Titus, "Pastoral Principles to Further Develop Hispanic Ministry," *¡En Marcha!* (Fall–Winter 2002): 13–14. The principles appear here verbatim from his article.

GLOSSARY

(La) Acostada del Niño—the family practice of enthroning a statue of the Child Jesus in the home at Christmas

(Las) Apariciones—usually refers to the dramatic reenactment of the apparitions of Our Lady of Guadalupe to the Indian Juan Diego

Arras—coins used in the marriage ceremony that symbolize a desire to provide on the part of the groom and a willingness to practice good stewardship on the part of the bride. Given that many women are now also breadwinners, this symbolism is sometimes altered today to speak of a more mutual role in providing material necessities for the household

(La) Candelaria—February 2, Candlemas Day, the feast of the purification of Mary and of the presentation of the Child Jesus in the temple

Chamba—colloquial expression for work, especially in the sense of temporariness or that which does not pay well

Chicano/a—Mexican-American; a term that was quite popular in the 1960s and 1970s

Como Dios manda (as God asks)—phrase used when describing something that is seen as God's will

Compadrazgo—sometimes translated as "godparentage"; usually involves a solemn commitment to the family as friend, confidant, and advisor, and a commitment to become a true "other parent" to the newly baptized child. The parents and the godparents of the child become *compadre* or *comadre* to each other

Criollo—the name given to a child of Spaniards born in the Americas. The Spaniards were known as *Peninsulares*

Cursillo—a "small course" in Christian life; refers to an intensive weekend retreat in which peer ministry is emphasized. The persons who promote such retreats and Christian fellowship are known as *Cursillistas*

(El) Día de los Muertos—November 2, All Souls' Day or the Day of the Dead

Día de los Reyes—January 6, celebrates the arrival of the Magi; traditionally the day for gift giving

Dichos or **refranes**—folk sayings or proverbs

(La) Dolorosa—Mary, the Sorrowful Mother

Flor y canto—"flower and song"; in Aztec philosophy and religion refers to the belief that only through flower and song can truth be grasped

Guadalupanismo—the following of or belief in Our Lady of Guadalupe; *Guadalupano/a* refers to the man (o) or woman (a) who can be a member of a certain confraternity

"Hermeneutical privilege of the poor"—hermeneutics has to do with the tools used to interpret a text; this phrase, popularized by some liberation theologians, refers to the special insights the poor have because of their marginalized and oppressed situation to interpret the Scriptures

Juramento—a solemn oath to abstain from some vice or habit for a certain length of time; while the person usually swears off alcohol, he or she may also give up smoking or drugs. This oath is made in the presence of one of the Church's ministers when the person is feeling overwhelmed by some addiction

Lasso—a type of rosary that is put over the shoulders of the bride and groom that signifies the life commitment they make to each other and the bond that will unite their lives and love

Luminarias—small brown paper bags filled with sand and lit candles that are prominently displayed along buildings and walkways on Christmas Eve; custom especially popular in New Mexico and West Texas

Luto—a period of mourning after the death of a loved one

Machismo—an attitude of male dominance

Mañanitas—an early morning serenade for a loved one, often done in honor of the Blessed Mother before the break of dawn on one of her feast days

Mestizo—traditionally used to designate a person who is a mixture of both indigenous and European blood. *Mestizaje* refers to the process

Milagrito or **exvoto**—types of testimonials that a certain petition was granted

(La) Misa de Gallo—midnight Mass on Christmas Eve

Misiones—a series of Lenten talks aimed at spiritual renewal usually done at the parish level; a mission

Mujerista theology—one of the forms of Latina feminist theology

Mulatto/a—a person who is a mixture of both white and African blood

Nacimiento—the Nativity scene

(El) Nazareno—the suffering Jesus

Novenario—family prayer rituals such as rosaries or the anniversary Masses for the soul of the deceased

Padrinos—godparents, sponsors, or marriage witnesses; *madrina* is the feminine form and *padrino* is the masculine form

"Pastoral de conjunto"—pastoral work done as a team; a pastoral focus and approach to action arising from shared reflection among the agents of evangelization

Pastorela or **Los Pastores**—a shepherds' play usually performed around Christmas

Pedir la mano—the custom of the parents of the groom going to ask the parents of the bride for her hand in marriage

Peregrinación—pilgrimage

(El) Pésame a la Virgen—a service held on the evening of Good Friday in which the community expresses its condolences to Mary, the Sorrowful Mother

Posadas—literally means an inn or hospitality; a Christmas novena that reenacts Joseph and Mary's search for lodging

Promesa—promise; has two basic elements: the petition of a favor and the *manda* or vow that is the fulfillment of stipulations accompanying the vow

Quetzalcóatle—the feathered serpent in ancient Mesoamerican mythology who is a symbol of fertility and life; creator of the human world, he gave human beings their tools and their crafts, and he taught them to polish jade, knit feathers, and plant corn. According to Aztec legend, this king-god was supposed to return to Mexico around the time of the arrival of the conquistador, Hernán Cortés

Quinceañera or **quince años**—a rite of passage or "coming of age" celebration for a young woman at fifteen years of age

Reconquista—the reconquest of Spain from the Moors

Recuerdos—mementos that are given out by a family after a baptism, wedding, or anniversary of death Mass

Semana Santa—Holy Week

Sensus fidelium—the sense of the faithful; the living witness of the faith of the people, that is, a certain "faith-ful" intuition that springs from a Christian way of life

(El) Sermon de las siete palabras—the sermon of the Seven Last Words that is preached on Good Friday afternoon; often lengthy reflections based on Jesus' words from the cross, usually interspersed with hymns and prayers

(El) Servicio del santo entierro—a solemn funeral procession featuring an image of the dead Christ

Teología de conjunto—the type of theology that comes out of a *pastoral de conjunto* (see above)

Veladora—a candle lit as an offering

Via Crucis—a live reenactment of the way of the cross or passion of Jesus

ABOUT THE AUTHOR

Father Eduardo C. Fernández, SJ, teaches pastoral theology and missiology at the Jesuit School of Theology in Berkeley and the Graduate Theological Union. A native of El Paso, Texas, he earned a doctorate in theology at the Pontifical Gregorian University in Rome in 1995. He is past president of the Academy of Catholic Hispanic Theologians of the United States (ACHTUS). His ministerial experience includes high school and university teaching, parish and campus ministry, and retreat work. Father Fernández is the author of numerous articles and several books.